(UNANSWERED)
SMOKE, MIRRORS, AND GOD

Nancy Fitzgerald

Published by CrossSection
940 Calle Negocio #175
San Clemente, CA 92673
800-946-5983
crosssection.com

Book + Jacket design by Crosssection
Set in Adobe Garamond, Font Bureau Agency, and Frutiger
First Edition: December 2014
Printed in the USA

ISBN 978-0-9899537-1-9 (paperback)
ISBN 978-0-9899537-2-6 (kindle)

Dedication

I am dedicating this book to my children – Scott, Mark, Andrew and Kelly and to my grandchildren – Kaitlyn, Sydney, Anabella, Jack, Edward, Austin, Lilly and Blake. The way you live and love one another, including your Lord, brings joy to my soul.

Contents

Foreword

If this were just another book about someone's personal religious agenda or ideas about God, this project would never have been written. Why? Because those books are a dime a dozen and the plot is usually disinteresting and always the same. What began as a life experience set in motion by a deeply personal tragedy for Nancy Fitzgerald, eventually morphed into a life long journey to objectively look into the notion of whether there is any type of God, religion or spiritual truth that can be verified and if so, why should anyone care. This has not been an easy undertaking when you consider the world's religions are vast, not in unison, and often at war with each other. Sadly, our research revealed that most of the people we interviewed typically go through the actions of fulfilling their list of religious obligations without knowing if or what they believe is true. Most just pointed to family tradition as their reasoning for their beliefs.

Why is there so much tension and hatred between conflicting beliefs both within and outside religious structures? None of them are exempt to strands of hatred, corruption, control, and abuse. Is there any wonder why atheism is a reasonable option to man's ridiculous and scandalous presentation of their God? Is there a true God who can be verified and through Him, can give us hope and courage to live in this broken world?

The statement that "we are all a product of our environment" is an overused idea to both justify and excuse ourselves from portions of our life that we would prefer to remain hidden or status quo. However, when it comes to the subject matter that we are digging into in this study, we found that the highest percentage of why people believe what they believe was inherited or borrowed from someone else. Whether it be parents, other family members or a geographic predisposition from birth, it is true that we most often align what we "say" we believe with what has been expected of us. But the question is: Do we really believe what we are saying?

According to our research, millions of people view religion and God as best summed up by "smoke and mirrors".

I am a product of my own religious environment and performance based routines that were as mandatory as my other chores. By the time I was in high school, my religion had formed a stage of clarity shaped from those early childhood years. It was clear to me that, yes, God was indeed angry with me for the mistakes I had made, but if I would ask Jesus into my heart, all would be well. Hopefully, it just might be enough to get me into heaven but as I learned through many Sunday school lessons - that was no "slam dunk". It was clear that Jesus was the only way to save me from God. That was my belief system for most of my life.

This study is not about me, however, my story is one that is replicated by thousands of people who have experienced the very same early thoughts about God or some higher power. There was absolutely no assurance that I mattered or that I had a higher purpose other than being a good person and living a moral life that was responsible. I had no proof of any hope beyond my own effort and futile attempts to live a perfect life.

As Nancy and I talked about this project, got into the research, and studied the Scriptures, I found that my own questions about God and life were being answered. Up until that point, I dared not ask tough questions for fear of judgment. I found out that there are real answers to my doubts and sufferings and that, with them, I can live fully even as a broken person in a messed up world. As a husband and father, I found and shared the material in this study with my wife and children. They too had many questions answered that had previously gone unanswered.

As a parent, we did not know much about what we believed to be true, so how could we teach our children with any real basis for believing in any type of God? This is why I am thrilled to be a part of this series. This study takes aim at the ideas, claims, testimony, scientific applications, archeological discoveries and other validated forms of unbiased investigation that have been used to shape the world's religions and their most important claims. As we tested this project with parents, most said that they wished that they had learned this material much earlier in life as they too had walked away from believing in any type of verifiable truth.

I am hopeful that the countless hours and years of study that have been applied to this project will afford each of you the necessary information and tools to resolve many of your questions that have gone UNANSWERED!

Doug Martinez
Chairman
Temporary Holdings, LLC

Acknowledgements

Because I have come from a life lived solely dependent on my own wits coupled with a worldview of which I was the center, any good that will come from my efforts, including this project, is a result of the grace extended by my Lord and Savior Jesus Christ. He was faithful to love and forgive me and call me His child when I put my trust in Him. He gave me an appetite for learning truth and then showed me the way to teach it to others. Fulfilling any call from God is far from easy, but to know that He has used someone like me to inspire others, who have questions and want honest answers about life, purpose, forgiveness, hope, suffering and death, is overwhelming. Thank you, Lord!

I am eternally grateful to my board and to my Christian friends and supporters. You have been faithful to pray, to help out whenever needed, and have given me wonderful advise, encouragement and resources. Thank you for sharing your wisdom as to how to run and develop an effective ministry as well as how to raise the bar in producing a life changing Christian Worldview curriculum.

To my husband Ed, my number one encourager, thank you for being willing to read and edit all of our material many times over! To Ashley Houston, for your patience and diligence in working alongside me in editing and making suggestions that made this project readable, I am grateful beyond words.

A final thank you goes to all those who are searching for answers to questions about God, life and how to better understand, communicate and love others the way God intended us to love. Thank you for choosing this curriculum. We hope and pray that this project will help you on your spiritual journey.

"Ask, and it will be given to you; seek, and you will find; knock, and it will be opened to you. For everyone who asks receives, and the one who seeks finds, and to the one who knocks it will be opened" Matthew 7:7-8.

CHAPTER ONE
THE LAKE

Chapter 1: The Lake

My earliest recollection of God was at Sunday school, where we played house, drank lukewarm milk, ate graham crackers, sang songs and listened to stories. At age 5, God was a conception that we sang about once a week. Outside of that, I had no thoughts about Him that affected how I lived or what I believed. All that, however, was about to change.

The moment the bell rang signifying the end of the school year, I, along with my two brothers and sister, were in our car on our way to our island home at "the lake." Otherwise known as Gull Lake in southwestern Michigan, it is a beautiful, crystal-clear, spring-fed lake with sandy shores and sunny skies. Life at the lake was good, very good. One day would flow into the next and soon it was time to move back into town and prepare to go to school once again.

There was, however, one day I will never forget. I was 5 years old and my older sister, Carole, was 7. We were in our yard engaged in a game of croquet while our two-year-old brother, Stephen, was in the house with our babysitter. My mother had gone into town, as she did every week, to do the laundry. My father was at work and my older brother, Joel, was at camp. Our playing was interrupted by a shout from our babysitter, "Where is Stephen?" "We don't know," we replied. "Carole, you go into the woods and look for him. Nancy, you look for him on the dock. I'll check in the house once again."

I went running out on the dock shouting his name, "Stephen, where are you? Steeeephen!" It was nothing new for Stephen to run off. He had done this several times before, and I kept thinking that any moment his blond, curly head would pop around the corner of the boathouse, flashing his big, toothy grin. I looked all over, but Stephen was nowhere to be found. Assured that he was not out there, I began to walk back down the dock toward the house. Something caught my eye by the shoreline. It was Stephen. He was floating face down in the water. I shouted to the babysitter and then jumped in, trying desperately to rescue him. I struggled to pick him up but being small myself; I couldn't budge him.

Within seconds, the babysitter leapt into the water and lifted him up in her arms. Water was streaming off his face and down his hair. His once active little body was still. "What's wrong with Stephen?" I asked. "He's dead, and it's your fault," she screamed. With that, she ran with Stephen in her arms, out of the water and to the neighbor's house. Carole and I were left alone to ponder what had just happened. It was the last time we saw him.

The next thing I can remember was our yard filling with many friends and neighbors. Some were crying loudly, while others stood and hugged each other. Friends surrounded my mother while my father sat in a chair with his head buried in his hands. I sat with my sister on the front steps, numb, empty and scared; there was no lap to sit in or arms to fall into. Alone, I retreated into the house to my parents' bedroom.

Like so many of us, my understanding of God was limited. We said grace before our dinner meal. At night, before bed, my father would come up stairs and we would always pray, "Now I lay me down to sleep. Pray the Lord my soul to keep and if I die before I wake, I pray the Lord my soul to take. Amen." The prayer always bothered me but I knew that God loved me, because the Bible told me so, at least that's what the Sunday school teacher said. I believed that God was probably good and could do anything. With that kind of childlike faith, I pleaded with Him.

"God, I know you can make Stephen better. Please fix him." There was nothing else to say. I knew God must be big and could help people. Stephen was just a baby, so of course He would fix him. Why not? Isn't that what God does?

With that, I went to be with my sister. After what seemed like an eternity, my father came and informed us that Stephen had died and was now in heaven with God.

"Why would he want to live with God, He didn't make Steven better?" I thought.

Alone and afraid, I retreated back into my parents' bedroom, and once again addressed God. "Why didn't you make Stephen live? I don't want to happen to me what happened to him. Maybe you're not good. You scare me. Stay away from me." At that moment, I walked out of the bedroom and away from God for the next 27 years.

A part of me died that day, as I think it did for many of us. For me, it was the end of the innocence of youth. Nothing was for certain any longer, not even God. I felt alone and scared of life and of death. "Why would my father be happy that Stephen was in heaven with God?" I reasoned, "He let him die!"

Life went on, as it does when tragedy happens, but my encounter with death and the guilt attached to it lingered for years to come. In those days, people generally weren't very good about processing traumatic events, and my parents were no exception. Very little was ever mentioned from that day on about Stephen, or about how we children were dealing with such a horrific tragedy. For whatever reason, Joel, Carole and I did not attend the funeral. We spent the rest of the week with our grandparents and then went back to the lake and were expected to live as if nothing had happened. For me, however, there were constant reminders of that dreadful day at the lake: my own guilt and Stephen's empty crib that remained in my bedroom for the rest of that summer. However, the emptiness of the crib did not begin to compare to the barrenness of my soul.

Several years later, I was sitting in my eighth grade science class. This particular day we were talking about the properties of water. I remember my teacher explaining to our class that although water was made up of hydrogen and oxygen, you still couldn't breathe while underwater. The next thing I remember was getting extremely lightheaded, and then I passed out. I was taken to the hospital and given a multitude of tests, but no one could figure out what was wrong with me. The next day, a friend of my parents, who was a child psychologist, came to visit me in the hospital. We chatted for a little while and then he asked me a question, "Do you ever think about Stephen?" I was shocked because no one had talked about him since the day he died. I had never been asked about how I felt about it. "Yes, I do," I responded, and then said very matter-of-factly, "You know, I killed him." I will never forget the look on Dr. C's face. "You what?" he said. "Nancy, look at me, you did not kill him. You were five years old, for God's sake. You were not the babysitter. You did not kill him! Hear me, you did not kill him!" More than his words of exoneration, the look of horror on his face gave me a huge sense of relief for the first time. At that very moment, I felt freed from the guilt over my brother's death. It was amazing, but the greater issue remained: "Who are you really, God? Are you real? Are you good or evil? Why would you kill a child?" I had no one to talk to, no one who could answer my questions. I did what so many of us do—I buried them in the deepest part of my soul and continued to live life as a "normal" teen, pretending that all was well.

I ended up attending and graduating from Indiana University with three degrees. I loved every minute of it, and would not have traded those experiences or friendships for anything in the world. However, toward the end of my college experience, I would often wonder, "What is my purpose in life? Is there a God?" In searching for answers, I would engage in conversations with all kinds of people from different backgrounds and with different beliefs about their purpose in life. From Christians to atheists, most of them said that their purpose was to make a lot of money, get a good job and enjoy life.

Through those times of questioning others, it was the group that called themselves "Christians" that I found to be both interesting and troubling. They all would acknowledge that they believed in God, but when I pressed them for the reason why they believed, or how they knew Christianity wasn't a hoax, not one of them could give me a reason that made sense. The answers were unbelievably shallow and pretty much the same: "I grew up that way." "It makes me feel good." "My parents told me so." I would ask over and over again for them to tell me the difference God had made in their life. Not one single person could do it. Not a single one!

I was frustrated and disgusted that highly educated people would identify themselves with Christianity, but have absolutely no idea if what they believed was true. In my soul I knew I needed God, but my mind was totally turned off. I became very cynical toward Christianity and toward Christians in general. My natural inclination was to conclude that this whole Christian thing was either a hoax or an extremely restrictive way of living for the weak minded. I came to the conclusion that my purpose in life was to have fun and take from life as much as I possibly could.

To my surprise, I met a guy who was one of the few people I had met during my college experience who thought about something other than the next weekend's party. Ed wanted to go to medical school and fulfill his dream of being a thoracic surgeon. He wanted his life to count. We continued to spend lots of time together through the next few years. We got to know each other's families and he and my dad became best friends. They went fishing and bird hunting together. That was a big deal for me because my dad and I were extremely close, and his approval of Ed was extremely important to me. After I finished my graduate studies and Ed completed his second year of medical school, we decided that we would get married, someday buy a house, have kids, play golf and live the "good life." Our plan seemed great, so we got married.

When Ed completed medical school, we moved to Hershey, Pennsylvania, where he began his surgical residency at the Hershey Medical Center. At that point, our dream of a perfect life began to take an unhealthy turn as we saw less and less of each other. He was on call almost every night at the hospital, so I decided I would play lots of tournaments and consider becoming a professional golfer. I traveled all over the country that year, playing in amateur and professional events, but soon decided that it was not the life for me. It was too difficult traveling in a car, staying in motels and constantly being with people with whom I had very little in common outside of golf. The game I loved became a chore, so I returned home with the desire of having kids and playing golf as an amateur. Our first son, Scott, was born, and 15 months later, our son, Mark, joined the family. Being a mom brought more joy and more anxiety to me, than I could ever have imagined. I loved the boys beyond words, and the thought of one of them dying was often at the forefront of my mind. I got up in the middle of every night to make sure they were breathing.

Finally, the residency was over and it was time to say good-bye to beautiful Hershey, and hello to a new life in Indianapolis. Now it was time for our dream lives to begin; we moved into a real home in a great neighborhood filled with kids! We had waited for this moment for the last eight years. I was going to raise the kids, play golf, get involved in the community, while Ed would join a medical group and perform heart and lung surgeries. He would be home at five every night, and we could begin to live out the American dream—a wonderful family and a happy marriage. At least, that was my plan.

My life and Ed's life became extremely busy: he, with his practice, and mine with raising our children. Within the next year and a half, I had given birth to our third son, Andrew, and then to our daughter, Kelly. I absolutely loved our kids and would do whatever it took to make sure that they were happy and healthy. I still continued my night vigil of checking to make sure that all four kids were breathing. My fear of them dying was overwhelming.

In spite of all the family and material blessings, in my heart there was no peace, purpose or joy. I felt empty inside. There was something very wrong. "Was this all there was to life?" I had tried to do everything right, but I still had no feeling of fulfillment. On the outside, we were living out the American dream, but to what avail? The one thing I did know was that happiness and peace and joy were not found in the material world, not in our jobs, our houses, our children, spouses or friends. Could it possibly be connected in any way to God? Was there a God? Might there be a God who could give me a little peace of mind and purpose? I began my search to find if there just might be a God who was different from the one that I had imagined Him to be as a young girl. I was desperate—I needed to find out for myself if there truly was a God who loved and cared for me.

What did the different religions have to say about God and about this person called Jesus Christ? Despite my bias against Christians, it was time for me to take a very serious look at Christianity and their holy book, the Bible, to see what it had to say about Jesus Christ.

Not long after my search for truth began, I made plans to go to Florida with some friends of mine to play in a golf tournament. I needed the rest and wanted to take some time to look into the Bible for the first time to see if it had anything to say about life and this person, Jesus. I packed a very skinny Bible because I figured that it was easier to read than a thick one. I arrived early and anxiously began reading the Bible from page one. Now was my chance to see what all this Christian stuff was about. My enthusiasm quickly waned; it didn't take me long to see that this book was confusing. I read through Genesis, glanced through some pages Exodus and slogged my way through the beginning of the book Leviticus. Frustrated, I came to the conclusion that there was no Jesus Christ in the Bible and God drowned people—once again those fears about God surfaced. Frankly, I found it all to be confusing and of little value in giving me the key to purpose, joy and hope in this life and the next, if there was one. I became discouraged as I realized that if there is no God, then there is no hope, and things for me were only going to get worse. "Who and where are you, God?"

"Ask and it will be given to you; seek and you will find; knock and the door will be opened to you. For everyone who asks receives; he who seeks finds; and to him who knocks, the door will be opened" (Matthew 7:7-8).

I stayed with a friend of mine, Cookie, who was one of those "born again Christians." I gathered up my courage and confided in her that I was searching for God or this Jesus, but could find nothing in the Bible that had made any sense to me. She lovingly told me that the Bible was made up of 66 books, and a good place to start was in the book of John. Not knowing what the book of John was, with love, encouragement and a lot of patience, she turned about three quarters through the Bible and showed it to me. I read it myself and by the end of the third chapter of John, God had begun to open my eyes and answer the questions I had been pondering since the day Stephen died. *"In the beginning was the Word, and the Word was with God, and the Word was God" (John 1:1)*. Who is the Word? Whoever He was, I knew He was eternal and I knew He was God. Then I read on down, *"But to all who did receive him, who believed in his name, he gave the right to become children of God, who were born, not of blood nor of the will of the flesh nor of the will of man, but of God. And the Word became flesh and dwelt among us, and we have seen his glory, glory as of the only Son from the Father, full of grace and truth" (John 1:12-14)*. Then I landed on the third chapter, *"For God so loved the world, that he gave his only Son, that whoever believes in him should not perish but have eternal life. For God did not send his Son into the world to condemn the world, but in order that the world might be saved through him. Whoever believes in him is not condemned, but whoever does not believe is condemned already, because he has not believed in the name of the only Son of God" (John 3:16-18)*. "That is it! This Jesus is the answer to life and He is the answer to death. Is it true?" I thought.

That evening, when everyone else had gone to bed, I once again began to pray to God. I simply told Him that I had no clue about who He really was, that I was lost and in great need of peace and joy. I told Him that if He were truly the God of the Bible, author of life and giver of peace, to invade my inner being, change my heart and give me peace and joy and love, which I so desperately needed. I informed Him that under no circumstance was I going to go to Africa, nor would I be any kind of the missionary type person, nor would I ever tell anyone what I just did. I was fearful that if He was really God, He might change me into one of those "weird Christians" for whom I had developed a pretty strong dislike. Giving up control did not sit well with me either, but I asked Him to show Himself to be real, and if He would do that, I would become an ardent follower of Him forever. I had no idea of what it meant to follow Jesus, but I was about to find out!

There are no words to explain what had happened to me, but I can tell you that my interest in playing in that particular golf tournament was gone; I could not wait to get home to my kids and to my husband. I came back on a major spiritual high. For the first time that I could remember, I was filled with a peace that I could not explain. I resumed my role as a mom and a wife, but with new excitement and energy. Ed began to notice a change. He said he thought I had gone on vacation to play some golf and hang out with the girls, but that I had come back a different person. He told me I left up-tight and anxious, and now there was a peace about me that he had never seen. Whatever it was, he said that he desperate-ly needed it himself. At that very moment, I knew that God was faithful to show Himself to me. He was who He said He was; He was God and He was alive in me!

I shared with Ed what I had found to be true about God, but that my journey had just begun. I told him that I knew very little about God, but that if he read the book of John that is about three quarters of the way through the Bible, he might begin to figure it out. Ed found a Bible and read the book of John, and he took the step of faith to trust Jesus as his Savior. Our new, but far from perfect, lives with Christ in the center of it all had begun. We both knew that we lived in a broken world that was filled with broken people. We were and continue to be those people. But as imperfect as we are, as rocky as our relationship can still be, God has proven over and over that He alone is faithful to show Himself to us and give us that peace and joy and life purpose for which we both yearned.

What amazed me the most was that, although our cir-cumstances did not change, no matter how difficult life was and will continue to be, God has been true to His word: He is the giver of peace and wisdom in the midst of very difficult times. Becoming a Christ follower does not mean that our lives will be perfect with no worries. In a broken world we all suffer, but God assures us that even in suffering He is with us and will help us persevere so that we might become more mature in our relationship with Him. God does not consult with me about the struggles coming in my life. He is God and I am not! This much I do know: we all suffer no matter who we are. We are all called to press on during hard times, no matter what. It isn't easy, but it builds character. There are many times that I have and still do feel like walking away from ministry, projects, and difficult friendships because it is just too hard. At those times, God, sometimes not so gently, reminds me that He never promised an easy life, that life is not about me or my comfort, that there is a reason for all things and that I need to trust Him in this. I am so grateful that God sustains me through these tough times because it makes me love and lean on Him all the more!

Soon after accepting Christ as my Savior, the first person that I thought of who really needed to know she is loved by God and that I have forgiven her completely for what was said to me the day Stephen died, was the babysitter. I prayed for her even though I didn't know her name. As God become more real to me through the Scriptures, I began to realize that my anger and unhealthy fear toward God had been replaced with a love and hunger to know Him more. Within weeks, I realized that I had slept through my nightly routine of checking to see if the children were breathing.

Believing that Jesus Christ died for me and rose again so that I and others who believe, could have life and have it to the full, signified just the beginning of my search to deepen my understanding of who this God is. I had questions that had been on my heart for years: Who is God? How can I know Him for sure? From where did I come and when I die, where am I going? Why is the world such a mess and, in the midst of that, what is my purpose in life? How can I be sure that the Bible stands alone and apart from all other books and is truly God's Word? Can I learn such things? My journey was one of looking for answers beyond emotions and opinions of others. I had to find out for myself what was true and separate from religion and man's imaginations and presuppositions. I was going to study the findings from other writers of antiquity, students of the Scriptures, archaeology, as well as the best thinkers of our time. Not only did I need to find answers for myself, but for my family, as well. They needed to know the truth about God so that they could live their lives with an assurance and hope—not the fear and anxiety that I carried around for all those years. God gave me a voracious appetite for knowing truth and for teaching it to anyone who would listen. Strangely enough, those feelings remain as strong today as they were then.

As our children grew up, I took great joy in praying for them and sharing with them some of what I was learning about this great God we worship. Ed and I tried to live out the Christian worldview on a daily basis as best we could. It was not so much what we did, but the attitude that God gave us to become better listeners, lovers of others and much more compassionate, still with much room for growth. We would get up early in the morning on weekdays and have a short Bible study with the kids, spending time praying for each other and giving thanks. Although none of us liked getting up so early in the morning, it became a special thing for our busy family to do. It drew us closer together to God and to each other.

When our oldest son, Scott, was preparing for college, I realized that even though we had tried our hardest to love him, pray with him, and read the Scriptures with him, he was far from ready, on a spiritual level, to go out on his own. He knew God and loved his family, but was clearly not ready to contend with the conflicting worldviews that he was about to encounter as he walked onto the college campus of his choice. That was when God began to birth in me the idea of taking the research that I had accumulated over the years from the questions I had about God and Christianity and write a curriculum. It was to be specifically designed for seniors in high school and college students, preparing them not only to defend what they knew to be true about God and the Bible, but to be a light of hope in a dark and broken world.

That was more than 20 years ago. Today, the curriculum, Anchorsaway, is being taught around the country and beyond. *"Unanswered: Smoke, Mirrors, and God"* is a version of the Anchorsaway curriculum that is designed for small groups from teens to grandparents, who would like to better understand the Christian faith, including what it means to be a Christian and how to love God and others in all of life. As a result, I hope and pray that you will enjoy this study and share it with others! ✈

CHAPTER TWO
THE SEARCH

Chapter 2: The Search

If Christ were to appear before you, what would you see? Would He be standing with outstretched arms ready to embrace you? Would He be pointing His finger at you? Or would He have His back to you? It should be no surprise that the vast majority of our understanding of God is not based on Scripture, but rather on personal experiences, the media, our friends, parents, the church, and our culture. This results in ideas and thoughts about God that are often distinctly different from those found in the Bible. Although our finite minds limit our ability to totally understand God, the Bible allows us to peak behind the curtain and catch a glimpse of who God says He is rather than who we think He might be.

Scripture is packed full of writings that beautifully reveal God's character. Yet, for most of us, God remains a mystery mainly because knowing God is not a top priority in our lives. Only 37 percent of self-proclaimed born again Christians read the Bible once a week, and that includes Sunday in church![1] Faith for many has turned into a smorgasbord of picking and choosing whatever we want to believe and discarding the rest. It is a bit like becoming our own god. Statistics support such claims; 71 percent of adults are more likely to develop their own set of religious beliefs than adopt those taught in a church, 61 percent of which are born again Christians.[2]

These statistics are consistent with many organizations that study trends in churches and those who sit in the pews. What their findings reveal are not only broken perceptions of God, mankind and life but confusion and frustration of people knowing what, if anything, to believe. In essence, their worldviews about God are broken. A worldview is the foundation from which people think, live, view life, and respond to the world around them. If our worldview is not based on a solid a foundation of truth, then our faith and our lives are on shaky ground. If we don't know God, then the way we live is left to our own efforts of trying to figure out who we are, what God thinks of us, and how we might survive in our messed up world.

In this book, we are going to take a closer look at world-views and what a life with God in the center might be like. Who does God say He is and what does He think of us? Scripture is clear about God's motivation for creating us and about why He chose to die for us all.

"...but God shows his love for us in that while we were still sinners, Christ died for us" (Romans 5:8).

"But God, being rich in mercy, because of the great love with which he loved us, even when we were dead in our trespasses, made us alive together with Christ—by grace you have been saved" (Ephesians 2:4-5).

"For God so loved the world, that he gave his only Son, that whoever believes in him should not perish but have eternal life. For God did not send his Son into the world to condemn the world, but in order that the world might be saved through him" (John 3:16-17).

Do you see it? God, motivated by amazing love, gave His Son Jesus to die for our sins and rise again, proving that He is God. What does He ask in return? He asks us to believe in Him and love Him and others. The goal? That we might, with God living in us, live out our lives full of hope, love, joy and purpose to God's glory.

God never has, nor will He ever, force anyone to believe in Him or to perform for Him. He offers a choice that we all have to make: to believe or not to believe. When we choose to believe, we become God's children and can know for certain that, when we die, we will live forever with God in Heaven. By His nature, He cannot love us any more than He does right this minute. Is it hard for you to pause for a moment and say out loud, "God loves me now, just as I am and He always will"? For many of us, that is a difficult exercise because we, as broken people, simply cannot love that way. Loving unconditionally or with such constant intensity is something that no human can do naturally. Only God can! *"I am God not man, the Holy One in your midst..." (Hosea 11:9).*

Unless Christ is actively living through us, we cannot love God and others as we should. Our only recourse, we think, is to perform. Performance is a means to fulfill an obligation or requirement, to accomplish something as promised or expected. It always involves an audience.[3] When placed in a faith context, it looks like this: "If I can be good and do enough good things, and if those good things outweigh the bad, then hopefully God will like me and let me into heaven." For many of us, our theology turns into a performance gig that has no end, leaves us totally exhausted, frustrated and lost. We end up going to church just to go, being on church committees because we think we have to say "yes," and pretending that all is well with us when it's not! Sadly, we are hoping that God will honor our efforts and be pleased with us, somehow making up for the bad things we have done.

When we do not know (or forget) God's truth, we ingest a lie that causes many of us to fall into the trap of performing for God in order to earn His love and approval. Bryan Chapell in his book, *Holiness by Grace,* writes, "After initially trusting in Christ to make them right with God, many Christians embark on an endless pursuit of trying to satisfy God with good works that will keep him loving them. Such Christians believe that they are saved by God's grace but are kept in his care by their own goodness. This belief, whether articulated or buried deep in a psyche developed by the way we were treated by parents, spouses or others, makes the Christian life a perpetual race on a performance treadmill to keep winning God's affection…While the Christian life can be characterized as a race, we persevere on the course God marks out for us not by straining to gain his affection but by the assurance that he never stops viewing us from the perspective of his grace. God continually offers us unconditional love and the encouragement that our status as his children does not vary even though our efforts do."[4]

Is it possible to develop a relationship with God over time that does not involve performing for Him? Remembering that we are imperfect and have been performance driven for all of our lives makes breaking our performance addiction very difficult. In fact, I doubt that it could ever be completely eradicated. But hopefully, as we walk with God over time, the desire to earn His love and affection will be replaced by accepting His love and affection as a gift of His grace.

Never, ever forget how much you mean to God. You are no accident: *"For you formed my inward parts; you knitted me together in my mother's womb. I praise you, for I am fearfully and wonderfully made. Wonderful are your works; my soul knows it very well. My frame was not hidden from you, when I was being made in secret, intricately woven in the depths of the earth. Your eyes saw my unformed substance; in your book were written, every one of them, the days that were formed for me, when as yet there was none of them"* (Psalm 139:13-16).

Know that He made you in His image and designed you to have a relationship with Him that is unique, loving and full of purpose. Your walk with God and how He plans to use you will be different from others you know, so be content—don't try to make your walk look like someone else's. When we get to know God better, and can trust Him with more and more of our lives, we will begin to reflect God by the way we live and love, not by pretending to be someone we are not. With a proper understanding of God, we will be set free to become to be a person of integrity who recognizes that we are just as broken as those around us with doubts and fears. Being who God created you to be is what matters to God. Christianity is not about performing for others, especially for God.

In my own life journey, I know that I would have believed in Christ a lot sooner if it weren't for "Christian" hypocrites. A hypocrite is someone whose actions are contrary to his or her stated beliefs. It is pretending to be what the person is not. The word hypocrite comes from the Greek word "hypokrisis" which means "an actor". I think this is why some of our friends and family might choose not to attend church or have anything to do with Christianity. Obviously, not all Christians are hypocrites, but many would agree that this is a problem in the majority of churches. I had a student who stopped coming to Anchorsaway because the girls in her small group, who were friendly and loving in our class, ignored her at school. When "religious" people turn a cold shoulder to those who are different from them outside of a religious setting, many who are seeking truth, turn a cold shoulder to God. Being religious at church, and loving to good friends but cold to those who don't fit our definition of being worthy to be our friend is not what it means to be a Christ follower. Not even close.

"You hypocrites! Well did Isaiah prophesy of you, when he said: 'This people honors me with their lips, but their heart is far from me; in vain do they worship me, teaching as doctrines the commandments of men'" (Matthew 15:7-9).

"Not everyone who says to me, 'Lord, Lord,' will enter the kingdom of heaven, but the one who does the will of my Father who is in heaven. On that day many will say to me, 'Lord, Lord, did we not prophesy in your name, and cast out demons in your name, and do many mighty works in your name?' And then will I declare to them, 'I never knew you; depart from me, you workers of lawlessness'" (Matthew 7:21-23).

God is calling us to not only be consistent in our love but also honest as to our own brokenness as human beings. Think, for a moment about what would happen if Christians committed to being honest and real about their struggles, doubts, fears and questions? All of us know that we have periods of doubt and questions when it comes to life, God, our future, and the purpose of living in a broken and hurting world. No human being has all the answers. We're not supposed to—that's God's job. God wants us to come to Him, unashamed, so that He can quiet our minds and hearts, speaking truth to us so that we develop a genuine faith.

"But from there you will seek the LORD your God and you will find him, if you search after him with all your heart and with all your soul. When you are in tribulation, and all these things come upon you in the latter days, you will return to the LORD your God and obey his voice" (Deuteronomy 4:29-30).

"Ask and it will be given to you; seek and you will find; knock and the door will be opened to you. For everyone who asks receives; he who seeks finds; and to him who knocks, the door will be opened" (Matthew 7:7-8).

It is unhealthy to push doubts or questions away. Gone unresolved, our personal doubts, fears and questions can make us bitter, angry, and often depressed. Processing all of our "stuff" against the backdrop of the One who is eternal and true, empowers us to become spiritually, mentally and emotionally healthy.

Several years ago, my son, Mark, came into my study one evening and asked, "What happens if I can't believe? I just can't make myself believe. I honestly doubt everything about God. I want to believe God, but I just can't." I was touched that he would admit his feelings about his faith, and furthermore that he wanted to talk about it. I assured him that his kind of doubt was a good thing and, in the end, would draw him closer to God, thus increasing his faith. I told him that God honors those who are honestly seeking after Him and that he should always feel free to ask questions and try to find answers from people or sources that he could trust. I assured him that God has a plan for him that is special and unique. I also encouraged him to read through the books of John and Ephesians to gain a better understanding of who Jesus is and who we become when we trust Him. By the end of our conversation, he was encouraged and was going to try reading the Bible, praying, and finding ways God was working in his life that he was overlooking. For him, the best thing that came out of our conversation was to learn it was okay to doubt and that God would meet him right where he was. We prayed together, asking God to increase his faith. Not surprisingly, God has been faithful to Mark to build in him a real and active relationship with Himself.

Imagine if Christians had the courage to break free from the comfort zones and pride and dared to be the people that God has called us to be without putting on an act to impress someone. What if our focus switched from us to God and His will for our lives? We all know people who are lonely, depressed or overwhelmed. What would happen if there was someone who could answer some of their questions and bless them by listening, loving and building a meaningful relationship with them? What if that someone is you? As we work through this study prayerfully, with the power and work of the Holy Spirit, we will become better equipped to make a difference as we live out our faith as lights in a dark and broken world. ✈

Unanswered

CHAPTER THREE
ALARMING REALITY

Chapter 3: Alarming Reality

I knew I should have packed earlier, but isn't that always the case? After a very long workweek, I was just happy to make my 6 a.m. flight out of Indianapolis. I found my window seat and was soon ready for some much-needed, uninterrupted sleep, with the added hope of an empty row. That plan was quickly dashed as two guys settled in next to me. I greeted both of them and closed my eyes, preparing for my nap. Within minutes after takeoff, the flight attendant stopped at our row and woke me up to activate my TV for free. My seatmates looked at me, but said nothing. A few moments passed and she returned and asked me if I would like a snack as well.

At this point, the guys objected, "Why does she get the free TV and snacks and we don't?"

"Because she flies with us a lot," she replied as she made her way down the aisle to serve other travelers.

"Excuse me, but what do you do?" asked the one on the aisle.

"I head up a ministry that asks questions like, 'How do you know what you believe about God is true?'"

"Are you saying that you are a Christian?"

"Yes!" I responded. "Would you call yourself a Christ follower?"

"I used to be one," he said.

Here was my moment of choice: Do I engage in a conversation with this guy and miss out on sleep? Besides, he has already ordered a beer and probably isn't going to want to engage in a conversation about God.

"Hi, my name is Nancy," I said and shook his hand.

"My name is Aaron," he said.

I turned to the poor guy in the middle who no doubt was figuring it was going to be a very long flight as well.

"My name is Doug," he said as I awkwardly shook his hand.

"Aaron, you said that you used to be a Christian. What does that mean?"

"I used to be in tune with God and pretty committed in our church where my grandfather is the pastor," he responded. "I went almost every week and helped out wherever I could. But, the more involved I got in the church, the more disillusioned I became with all the hypocrisy—it made me doubt everything. I didn't know what to do, so I left the church and my faith in God. I know I really hurt my grandfather though, and I feel really bad about it."

"I'm sorry, Aaron, but what happened to you is not all that unusual. Many, like you, walk away from God, not because of God Himself, but because of some 'Christians' who misrepresent Him by misbehaving or by saying things that are simply not true. They pretend to be religious and speak for God, but they don't. There's no question that God was grieving with you over the hypocrisy in your church. Are you feeling like God has turned away from you and is angry with you for leaving?"

"Yes," he said tearfully. "I feel horrible about all of it."

"Sometimes our emotions deceive us into believing lies about God and ourselves. It happens to all of us. But this much I can promise you: God has never stopped loving you. You may have tried to walk away from Him, but He never left you! Do you believe that Christ died on the cross for the forgiveness of all your sins and rose again?"

"Yes."

"Then you are a Christian, whether you attend church or not. The Bible says that God will always be with you forever. Scripture also says that once you believe, you are adopted, sealed and redeemed from the guilt of your sin. Aaron, you are God's child. You can't un-adopt yourself! You were created in His image so that you could have a personal and vibrant life with God. He created you with purpose for His own pleasure. He has not turned from you nor has He given up on you. His arms are wide open waiting for you to simply turn back to Him."

"For some reason, I believe what you are saying is true. I have a lot to think about." With that, Aaron finished his beer, put his seat back and closed his eyes.

"Well," I said looking at wide-eyed Doug. "What's going on with you? Do you believe in God?"

"No," he said bracing himself.

"Well, once again, it obviously isn't because of God. So, who caused you to not pursue a faith in God?"

"When I was in junior high, a friend of mine invited me to a weekend at a Christian camp. I went, and the leader told us that if we didn't believe in God, we were going to hell."

"That was it? He didn't talk about how God loves you, Doug, and wants to have a relationship with you?"

"No."

"He didn't tell you that you matter to God, and that He wants you to believe in His Son Jesus who died and rose again, paying the price for your sins and proving that He is God?

"No."

"Once again, Doug, allow me to apologize for people that might be well meaning, but instead dump half truths on people like you that cause a lot of suffering. How old are you?"

"32."

"So, let me get this straight. For the last 20 years you haven't considered the possibility of God existing because you felt that God wanted nothing to do with you and that you were headed to hell?"

"Yeah, pretty much. I've known people who go to church, but no one talked about God to me. What you've said today—I've never heard before."

By this time, the plane was approaching our destination so our remaining time was short.

"I hope you will take some time to think about what we've talked about this morning. What I've shared isn't just my opinion; it's the truth because it comes directly from the Bible. Do you know a Christian who you could trust to talk to and get some honest answers about who God is and who you are in the eyes of God?"

Doug thought for a moment. "Yeah, I do know of a guy with Cru who leads a group on our campus. I can talk with him!"

"Terrific," I said, "He should be able to answer your questions or know someone who can. Are you a professor?"

"Yes."

"Have you had Christian students that you know of in your class?"

"Probably, but I've never really engaged in a conversation with them. Being a Christian on our campus is frowned upon."

"Well, maybe after you talk with your friend from Cru, that might change a bit."

"Maybe," he smiled.

The pilot came on and announced that we were about to land. With that, Aaron opened his eyes and moved his seat up and looked over at me.

"I am getting myself back with God. I'm also going to see my grandfather. You have no idea how grateful I am to have talked with you. I think my whole life is going to change. I'm excited to get back on road with Jesus. How can I thank you?"

"This isn't me," I said. "God is good about arranging seating assignments especially on planes. This was simply His way of telling you that He still loves you and wants you back. He has plans for you! Besides, I enjoyed meeting you guys."

Doug chimed in, "I promise that I'm going to talk with my friend so I can get myself straightened out too."

With that, the plane landed. We said our goodbyes and continued on our journeys, none of us the same.

This is one of hundreds of conversations that I have had over the years with people who have either walked away from their faith in God or who are agnostics, but are still searching for hope and meaning in a broken world that has nothing eternal to offer them. What can we, as the Church, those who would call themselves Christ followers, do to keep others and ourselves from abandoning our faith in God? What would happen if Christians were so well grounded in the foundations of their faith that Christ would no longer be stuff that we do, but would actually become a part of our DNA? Might that kind of authentic faith free us to love God and others in a real and powerful way? Might others see Christ in us without a word spoken? What if we were all prepared to engage in conversations about God with those we meet along our own life journey? Could we make a difference in the lives of others who are searching for God because we took the time to love them just as they are? Might we be used by God to cause others to rethink who He is and what their real purpose is in life?

Today the Church is in trouble. We have lost our saltiness and sadly, we have little, if any, influence in making a difference for Christ in our day-to-day activities. Fewer than 2 percent of us can verbalize the reason for the hope that we have in Jesus. Only 4 percent of us actually live out our faith on a daily basis, and a mere 9 percent of us believe in moral absolutes. Few Christians understand the difference, on a daily basis, that Christ's death and resurrection make in our lives. More than half of those who believe in Jesus as their Savior still think that He sinned while on earth and that a "good" person can earn their salvation. The most tragic of all of these statistics is the fact that up to 80 percent of all self-proclaimed Christians will leave their faith in God by the time they graduate from college.[1] Their faith is not strong enough to stand up against the pressure and intimidation that comes from their professors, from other students and from the world. That number encompasses many individuals we know, including our children, extended family and maybe even ourselves!

Why does all of this matter? Isn't it enough if people go to church, are nice to one another and work hard at their job? What else would God would want us to do?

One day the Pharisees approached Jesus with a question: *"'Teacher, which is the greatest commandment in the Law?' And he said to him, 'You shall love the Lord your God with all your heart and with all your soul and with all your mind. This is the great and first commandment. And a second is like it: You shall love your neighbor as yourself. On these two commandments depend all the Law and the Prophets'" (Matthew 22:36-40).*

I am convinced that God is far less concerned with how often we attend church, Bible studies, and religious committee meetings or how hard we work at our jobs. Instead, God looks at our heart. What matters to Him is how we love Him and others. Notice in this verse that our devotion to Him should take place in our heart, soul and our mind. To intentionally love others means to engage, sometimes sacrificially, in the lives of those we meet along our way.

Building a solid foundation of the Christian faith is what this project is all about. It's a journey that will help develop a deep trust in God who can empower you to be a light to others. We hope that through this study, your own questions about God, about how He views you and His purpose for you might be more fully realized. Then you can fulfill what God has designed you to be: His child, His friend, and His hands and feet wherever you go!

"...so that we may no longer be children, tossed to and fro by the waves and carried about by every wind of doctrine, by human cunning, by craftiness in deceitful schemes. Rather, speaking the truth in love, we are to grow up in every way into him who is the head, into Christ" (Ephesians 4:14-15).

Unanswered

CHAPTER FOUR
PERFORMANCE TRAP

Chapter 4: Performance Trap

Have you ever gone into a movie well after it has started? It happens to me on a fairly regular basis. It takes only a moment to annoy everyone around when I start asking questions so that the story on the screen makes some sense. I want to know who the main characters are and if they are they the good or bad guys. I also want to know the story that has led up to my entry point so that I can enjoy the rest of it with all the others. Had I been on time like all the rest, it would have been easier on everyone, including myself.

Coming to a belief in Christ at 32 years of age, I had some serious catching up to do! I had a million questions, which I am sure annoyed those around me because I didn't want to leave a single rock unturned when it came to the building blocks of my newfound faith. It did not take me long to realize that there is diversity in what Christians believe to be true about God. Some thought He was personal while others saw Him as distant. Some experienced His love and forgiveness and others believed He was judgmental and demanding. Some thought they were a god while others doubted the possibility of only one true God.

Why all the confusion about God? After all, I thought, we are one nation under God! How could a Christian nation lose its focus and turn away from God on so many fronts? I quickly learned you do not have to wear a black robe with a collar to preach about God. In our culture, some of the most persuasive preachers about their "god" are teachers, scientists, writers, television news anchors, movies, movie stars, musicians, artists or perhaps even your best friend. The list is unending.

In a sense, all of us are preachers. The way we think, interact with one another, and voice our opinions about the people and things in our lives, all set the stage for our "sermons." For me, because I didn't believe in the God of the Scriptures, I lived according to my own set of rules and I decided what was right and wrong. Life, simply stated, was all about me. Being successful, accepted and materially comfortable was my focus, and therefore, everything I said and how I lived reflected my own "me-centered" goals in life. If there was a God, I figured that He graded on a curve. I never killed anyone, and I volunteered to serve at a church brunch once, so surely I was "in". Without saying a word, I was preaching to everyone I met. No, I wasn't standing on a street corner yelling at people, but I was preaching my beliefs by the way I lived, by my moral convictions and by how and what I communicated to others. I was simply living out a Godless worldview.

Worldviews are similar to wearing a pair of glasses. We all wear them. The color of the lenses in our glasses determines how we see things. If you have a pair of glasses with blue lenses in them, everything will look blue. Wearing a pair of glasses with red lenses will cause everything to appear red. What we believe in our hearts to be true will determine how we live and how we see and interact with the world around us. We reflect our worldview by the way we speak, dress, spend money, love others, work at our jobs and live out our life in general.

As there are many different colors of lenses from which to choose, there are just as many worldviews. The ones we are going to study in this book are: the Christian worldview, the Naturalist/Humanist worldview and the Postmodern worldview. No one person lives strictly within a worldview, but his or her foundational beliefs will generally fall into a particular category or worldview.

Our approach to the study of worldviews is to see how each one answers the basic questions that most of us have. They are: From where did I come? Why is there such a mess in the world? Is there any hope? What is my purpose here on earth? What happens when I die?

Does the Christian worldview answer these questions in a way that makes sense, is transformational and verifiable? What about the other worldviews? How do they answer those life questions? Studying the other worldviews is extremely valuable because it reinforces the importance of understanding why we think and live the way we do. We can also learn how to better understand from where people are coming philosophically, along with how we might better communicate with those who think and believe differently than we do.

The Christian worldview embraces the following truths: The Bible is the inerrant, inspired Word of God and is the "handbook" for living the Christian life. It accepts the book of Genesis that tells the history of how God created the universe and everything in it! It also tells the beginning of man's sinfulness and how sin separates man from our holy God. The relationship between sinful man and a holy God is solely restored through the redemptive work of Jesus Christ (through His death and resurrection). Salvation comes only as a gift from God, not through man's good works. Because Christ died for us, we have the privilege of living for His glory, through the power of the Holy Spirit, in all we do, say, and think.

The Bible reveals that God created men and women in His image so that we could have a personal relationship with Him. We were made with free will, a sense of right and wrong and a yearning to know God. Man was created with the need to love and to be loved, and Jesus Christ is the only One who can fill that need. The genuine Christian will be changed from the inside out through the work of the Holy Spirit, who dwells in all those who choose to believe in the Jesus of the Bible. The Spirit gives what all of us are looking for, but what none of us can experience outside of God: love, joy, peace, patience, kindness, goodness faithfulness, gentleness and self-control!

How does the Christian worldview answer the life questions?

1. From where did I come?

Scripture says that, in the beginning of time, God created the world and everything in it (Genesis 1). God created us all in love with purpose (Psalm 139).

2. Why is there such a mess in the world?

All of us, beginning with Adam and Eve, have rebelled (sinned) against God. Since that time, we have all been born separated from a relationship with God. We live for ourselves instead of living for Him (Genesis 3, Romans 3:23, 5:12). When we choose to disregard God and His standard for us, we invite trouble. Sin, when taken to fruition, goes from moral decline to total chaos, which ultimately leads to death. The Bible tells us *"after desire has conceived, it gives birth to sin; and sin, when it is full-grown, gives birth to death" (James 1:15).* We see the effects of sin in our culture today in some of the following examples: massive moral decline in the family, marriage, culture, media (internet, music, movies, television), wars, politics, schools, churches and businesses.

3. What hope do I have?

Jesus Christ, God's Son, came to earth ensuring that the penalty of every sin (past, present and future) has been paid for by Christ's death and resurrection. When I die, I will live forever in Heaven with God (John 3:16; Romans 10:10-11; 1 Corinthians 15:3-4). Salvation comes not through good works, but only through the gift of God's grace (Ephesians 2:8-9).

4. What is my purpose in life?

My purpose on earth is to love God, to love others, and to live life to the fullest (Matthew 22:36-40; John 10:10). My goal is to imitate God in what I do, say, and think. As I live my life in Christ, I can, through the leading of the Holy Spirit, be a voice of encouragement to those who are hurting and struggling in life.

5. What happens when I die?

Those who believe in Jesus Christ will live forever with Him in heaven (John 3:16, 14:2-3; Revelation 21:1-4).

At its heart, the Christian faith is about transformation, both in one's personal life and in our culture. The Christian worldview is like our DNA and should influence every facet of our lives and cultivate within us the desire to reach our world with the truth of the Gospel. When it comes to defending our faith: *"always be prepared to give an answer to everyone who asks you for a reason for the hope that is in you; yet do it with gentleness and respect"* (1 Peter 3:15).

A well-grounded understanding of the Christian worldview, therefore, is critical if we are to be able to constructively engage those who hold different worldviews. The better we know our own Christian faith, the easier it will be for us to recognize those who make false claims regarding truth. By knowing and living out the Christian worldview, we will be able to defend our faith when it is challenged by others and be a light of hope that draws others to an authentic relationship with Jesus. ✈

CHAPTER FIVE
FIGHT CLUB

Chapter 5: Fight Club

My mother was no better of a cook than me. She will forever be remembered for her grilled cheese sandwich that was always burned (dark brown she would insist) and placed on the plate, burned side down. Another favorite dish of hers was what she called, "Garbage Veto." She would throw previous night's disasters like salmon, a roast, meatloaf, and chili together in a big pan, add potatoes and plenty of ketchup. Needless to say, she had few takers for dinner on those nights—we all made sure that we had other plans! The only lasting value to a Veto night is that it defines the Postmodern worldview to a tee.

Postmodernism is a conglomeration of other worldviews filled with contradictions that can, and often do, ultimately lead to disaster. Postmoderns do not believe in a transcendent God, but they do believe in total freedom in thought and action, making everyone their own "god" with abhorrence to any accountability or criticism. As far as the concept of truth, they adopt Nietzsche's philosophy, "There are no facts, only interpretations..."[1]

They choose morals that they value for themselves, which might be different from what others value. They say that they are totally tolerant of all people and all religions, except for Christianity with its belief in absolute truth. Free will, reason, and conscience are illusions, while pride and ignorance drive this worldview. They deny being a worldview because they like being undefined. Their favorite word is "whatever," which also reflects their attitude and behavior.

The term "Postmodernism" was first used in the 1930s, but it did not become truly established until the 1970s, first in the area of architecture, and then expanding into the rest of American culture. It grew out of Modernism, the late-19th-, early-20th-century trend that rejected tradition in favor of innovation and experimentation. The solution was to contend that there is no grand narrative, only a variety of differing perspectives of the world, all of which have equal value.

"The Postmodern heartbeat has pumped cynicism through the veins of our culture; we are distrusting of almost everything. There is no truth, no meaning, and no certainty. Yet, even in such a distrusting worldview, trust of the self is the one thing that seems to be left unquestioned. Why is this? When God is dead, someone or something will take His place. Someone will always be Lord. Self, interpretation, and taste are the rulers of the Postmodern worldview. Trusting your heart has become the religion of choice. But the question is this: Can you trust your heart simply because it feels? Can you trust your eyes simply because they see?"[2]

"For a time is coming when people will not endure sound teaching, but having itching ears they will accumulate for themselves teachers to suit their own passions, and will turn away from listening to the truth and wander off into myths" (2 Timothy 4:3-4).

The downside to this worldview is beyond words. They embrace feelings to guide them instead of truth. Feelings are gifts from God, but can also mislead those who completely rely on such a subjective system. Those who live out these precepts create chaos for themselves and others. Postmodernism, in its purest form, leads to a life without hope. It reflects a pessimistic view that everything is meaningless (nihilism). Mankind was created for purpose and hope, but Postmodernism brings about withdrawal, depression, hopelessness, and confusion that oftentimes leads to spiritual death and suicide. Many are heavily involved in the drug culture.

"For they exchanged the truth of God for a lie, and worshiped and served the creature rather than the Creator, who is blessed forever. Amen" (Romans 1:25).

How does the Postmodern answer the life questions?

1. From where did I come?

The universe created itself. I am the result of random, impersonal, undirected forces of nature. I did not come from a transcendent Creator God. Humanity is the result of purposeless evolutionary development over millions of years.

2. Why is there such a mess in the world?

There is nothing in which we can put our trust, since absolute truth is non-existent. People who advocate universal truths are the source of all the problems in the world. Their belief in absolutes results in power struggles.

3. Is there any hope?

There is nothing we can put our trust in, since absolute truth is non-existent.

4. What is my purpose in life?

We must each continually challenge everything in our world, applying the postmodern practice of deconstruction. We reject the idea of truth. We must also be tolerant of everything but Christianity.

5. What happens when I die?

The human body experiences physical death and nothing more beyond this life.

There is no doubt that Postmodernism is the predominant worldview today. Many churches have become "seeker friendly" to the point of abandoning truth in an effort to make people feel good and fill the coffers. As a result, those who come to church to learn about God often don't. Those who want to learn more about Christianity and what it means to love God and love others often go home empty. Is it any wonder that they eventually end up believing that Christianity is a show and that there is no such thing as truth?

CHAPTER SIX

OH MY GOD

Chapter 6: Oh My God

Several years ago, my friend, Cookie, and I were going to play in a golf tournament in Florida. We had not seen much of each other for a long time and were looking forward to catching up. The flight was packed. We found the way to our row and to our pleasant surprise, it was empty, which was a very good thing! I slid over to the window seat and Cookie took the aisle, leaving the middle seat vacant. We could not get over our good fortune. The flight attendant announced that the main door would soon be closed.

"Isn't it just like God to give us such a wonderful gift to sit in a row with just two of us? God is good!" I said.

At that moment, the last passenger stumbled on the plane. It didn't take long for everyone to realize that this guy had way too much to drink. He weaved his way down the aisle and paused by our row.

"You're in my seat," he exclaimed. "Move!"

"Lord," I whispered to myself as I exited my seat, "I hope You don't mind if I take back that last little bit of thanks I sent to You a few minutes ago."

Our new seatmate, Jim, literally fell into the window seat, leaving a waft of whiskey behind him. I took one look at Cookie and knew that she was not going to give up her aisle seat, so I settled into the dreaded claustrophobic middle seat. Soon we were off, and Cookie and I began sharing what God was doing in our ministries and in our lives. For several minutes, we were completely immersed in our conversation until, unexpectedly, Jim tapped my shoulder and said,

"Can you help me?"

"Excuse me," I said, somewhat annoyed to be taken away from my time with Cookie, "What do you mean, 'Can I help you?'"

I was expecting something cynical, and was wondering what on earth I was going to do, being wedged in a packed plane, with no place to move. I soon realized though that this was no laughing matter as his voice wavered and tears began to flow.

"My name is Jim. I have been listening to you and your friend. Maybe you can help me." "What's wrong?" I said, as I turned toward Jim, no longer aware of the smell of alcohol or the awkwardness of the situation.

"Yesterday, I got a phone call that my son dove into a pool and broke his neck. He's now paralyzed." He started to openly weep. "I don't know what to do. I don't know what to say to my son. Can you please help me?"

I quickly began asking God to give me the words that he needed to hear.

"I am sorry, but I cannot help you. I can't give you the peace that you need, nor can I give you the strength and the words that you need to communicate with your son. However, I do know Someone who can."

"Who is it?" he asked expectantly.

"His name is Jesus. He is the only One who can give you the wisdom and peace that you need. In the midst of this very difficult journey, I promise you that God will work through all that you are faced with today and in the days to come. Please know and believe that God loves you and God loves your son. He knows you both by name. He wants to walk through this with you and your son. He wants to bless you in ways you have never dreamed."

We talked for some time. I learned a lot about his family, where he lived and worked. He was a nice guy who was overcome with fear and grief, and his way of dealing with the pain was by drinking. Jim had gone to church and had some knowledge of God, but had never considered God to be personal, forgiving, or loving. Jim had many unanswered questions.

When I travel, I like to carry a small paperback New Testament Bible with me, in case God arranges time with someone who needs some encouragement. I reached into my carry-on, pulled it out and turned to the book of John. We talked about Jesus: being the Word and our only source of hope. I shared with him God's love for all mankind, and His promise that whoever believes in Him will not perish, but will have everlasting life with God in heaven! (John 3:16). I talked about the faithfulness of God and His promise never to leave him.

"God will never force Himself into someone's life. If you choose to believe in Him, He will take up residency in you."

"I believe," Jim said, before I had a chance to finish the sentence.

"Do you believe all that I have told you about Jesus is true?"

"Absolutely," responded Jim.

"Let's pray together," I said, as I took hold of his hand. "I will pray and then, if you want, you can quietly pray with me. OK?"

"I'm ready," said Jim in his loud voice, as he began to sob. Although I had just met him, I knew he was more than ready to confirm his faith in God through Christ.

I began to pray quietly with him, and he repeated what I was saying, with sobs growing louder and louder. Our area of the plane became extremely quiet. (Only God knows who else was praying along!) We continued praying and I thanked God for arranging this moment with Him. Jim affirmed that he believed in Jesus and asked for help. He prayed with words from the deepest part of his soul.

Jim became a believer that day. His situation had not changed, but he had. He was still flying to Florida to see his son who would, most likely, never walk again. Now, by the grace of God, Jim had hope and the outward appearance, as well as the inward confirmation, of peace. He promised that he would read the book of John at least three times and talk to some of his Christian friends about the commitment that he had made that day. He put the Bible in his shirt pocket and said,

"I can't wait to tell my son about this! We have so much to talk about!"

The plane landed and Jim couldn't wait to get on his way. I gave him a hug and off he went to be with his son.

Oh yes, about Cookie. She was a mess; she had been crying right along with Jim. She prayed for both of us while we were talking. I thank God for her support! As we were deplaning, I had some business to attend to with a friend of mine.

"Lord, about my taking back my thank You for the empty seat…Thank You, Lord, for using me in spite of my selfish self. You are a most loving and merciful God. Please be with Jim, his son and his family as he continues on his difficult journey. I love you."

We have all experienced suffering. Some is catastrophic, and others less life changing. One moment all is well, and in an instant, the horror of the brevity of life is looking at us in the face. An earthquake, a tsunami, war, disease, an accident, divorce, betrayal—where are You, God? The problem of suffering is perhaps the most difficult challenge a Christian will face in trying to understand how it aligns itself with the nature of a loving God. Scripture teaches that He is all powerful (omnipotent) and all loving (omnibenevolent). Thus the question, "Knowing that God could stop anything that is impeding our happiness and health, why does He allow it? Why does He allow us to suffer? Why?"

In working through these questions, it is essential to see what the Bible has to say about suffering. We can learn much if we go to the beginning of the Bible, to the book of Genesis. *"In the beginning God created the heavens and the earth" (Genesis 1:1).* In Genesis 1:3-25 God tells us the order of His creation and that it was all "good." In Genesis 1:26, God made male and female in "our image" and said in verse 31 that it was "very good." The two people that God created, Adam and Eve, lived in the Garden of Eden. All was well. Adam and Eve walked with God and communicated directly with Him. There was no suffering or death. It was like heaven on earth. So what happened?

God did not create robots. He created humans in His image, so that God could love us and we in turn can love Him. He wants to have fellowship with us, bless us, and give all mankind life to the full. God wants to call us friend. True love, God's love, requires choice. God chose to first love mankind, but did not force mankind to love Him in return. In Genesis 2:16-17, God introduced Adam to choice and the consequences of bad choices, when He told him that, *"You are free to eat from any tree in the garden; but you must not eat from the tree of the knowledge of good and evil, for when you eat of it you will surely die."* For the first time in Adam's life, he had to choose between right and wrong, good and evil, God or self. Was he going to obey or disobey God? With choice comes free will.

In Genesis 3:1-6, Satan, the serpent, introduces himself to Adam and Eve and immediately plants a seed of doubt by saying, *"'Did God really say...?'"* This is how Satan works—he plants doubt, and will always misrepresent the truth of God. Here we see Satan informing Adam and Eve that God would not judge them to death for their disobedience. Satan also lies about the very nature of our merciful and generous God by insinuating that God withholds from Adam and Eve (and future mankind) those things that are beneficial and make them feel good. First Eve, and then Adam, disobeyed God and believed Satan, the serpent. At that moment, the first sin was committed; fellowship between God and all mankind was broken from that moment on. Adam and Eve then began the spiritual and physical death that God had warned them about. They did not suddenly fall over dead, but the aging process began and continued until the physical end of their lives.

Today, many of us tend to take sin lightly, thinking that it is not a big deal because everyone does it. Don't underestimate the devastation and power that sin has in our lives. Sin is a terrible thing! It not only brought about death and the curse on all of mankind, but also, because of its terribleness, corrupted creation itself. *"The ground will produce thorns and thistles and man will eat from the plants of the field" (Genesis 3:18).* It is the source of all death and suffering that comes through the natural order, including disease, tornadoes and other natural disasters (Romans 8:20-22). We have no idea how horrific sin is when compared to the holiness of God. Though we might see it as no big deal, God views it quite differently.

"All have sinned and fallen short of the glory of God...the penalty for sin is death" (Romans 3:23, 6:23).

"Therefore, just as sin entered the world through one man, and death through sin, and in this way death came to all men, because all sinned" (Romans 5:12).

Before we think that God was too harsh in His judgment, note that in Genesis 3:15, God provides hope. It is found in the first prophecy—God promises a Messiah who would come and take away the penalty of the sin of the world by dying for us! For Adam and Eve, God handed out consequences for the sin that was committed. For all women, it was pain in childbearing (Genesis 3:16-17). For the man, he would painfully work all the days of his life.

As a result of sin, we as humans, are sinners both by nature and by choice. We live in a world that is broken filled with broken people. We can simply read news reports or watch television to see that mankind is very capable of doing evil things to one another, things that bring about much suffering. C.S. Lewis, author of, *The Problem of Pain,* estimates that 80 percent of all pain is caused by human agents.[1]

We do great damage to one another: physically, mentally, emotionally and spiritually. I think that we all can agree that by nature, we are incredibly selfish and want things to go our way. One person's sin can cause many of us to suffer, sometimes in ways that we never fully recover from. None of this is a surprise to God—we all suffer—but in the midst of it, He offers this encouragement:

"I have told you these things, so that in me you may have peace. In this world you will have trouble. But take heart! I have overcome the world" (John 16:33).

"Do not let your hearts be troubled. You believe in God; believe also in me" (John 14:1).

"Peace I leave with you; my peace I give you. I do not give to you as the world gives. Do not let your hearts be troubled and do not be afraid" (John 14:27).

God can and often does allow suffering because it brings us closer to Him. It is through suffering that most of us realize that we simply cannot "fix it" ourselves—we need some big time help to get us through. As we go to God in moments like this, He hears us and is glad that we have come to Him.

No doubt this is how God has designed us to be with Him on a daily basis. Since we are born with such a strong desire to do our own thing, we often miss out on the very essence of love, joy and peace, which can only come from God. He does not desire for you to hurt or to suffer for no reason. He does not desire for you to be in pain for pain's sake. What He does desire is for you to know the all surpassing greatness of His love, which will allow you to live life to the fullest in the midst of joy and suffering!

"I am the vine; you are the branches. If you remain in me and I in you, you will bear much fruit; apart from me you can do nothing" (John 15:5).

"…to comfort all who mourn, and provide for those who grieve in Zion—to bestow on them a crown of beauty instead of ashes, the oil of joy instead of mourning, and a garment of praise instead of a spirit of despair. They will be called oaks of righteousness, a planting of the Lord for the display of his splendor" (Isaiah 61:3).

Is the end result of suffering always evil? No! We grieve the death of a friend or family member. But although we grieve the loss of the Christian who dies, we can also celebrate death because we know he or she is finally free of suffering and is living in heaven because of faith in Jesus Christ. For them, there is no longer pain, no tears, and they will live forever in complete peace and joy with Jesus. The truth of the matter is, if they had a choice to come back to earth or stay in heaven, there is no question that they would stay in heaven. In our wildest imagination, we have no idea how incredibly awesome heaven is until we get there!

C.S. Lewis said, "Pain insists upon being attended to. God whispers to us in our pleasures, speaks in our conscience, and shouts in our pain. It is His megaphone to rouse a deaf world."[2]

Jesus Christ, who was on earth as 100 percent man and 100 percent God, embraced suffering. To suffer and die for our sins was His destiny. Keep in mind as you read this that Jesus was without sin, but was still willing to go through extreme suffering so that you could become His child.

"Who has believed our message and to whom has the arm of the LORD been revealed? He grew up before him like a tender shoot, and like a root out of dry ground. He had no beauty or majesty to attract us to him, nothing in his appearance that we should desire him. He was despised and rejected by men, a man of sorrows, and familiar with suffering. Like one from whom men hide their faces he was despised, and we esteemed him not. Surely he took up our infirmities and carried our sorrows, yet we considered him stricken by God, smitten by him, and afflicted. But he was pierced for our transgressions, he was crushed for our iniquities; the punishment that brought us peace was upon him, and by his wounds we are healed. We all, like sheep, have gone astray, each of us has turned to his own way; and the LORD has laid on him the iniquity of us all.

He was oppressed and afflicted, yet he did not open his mouth; he was led like a lamb to the slaughter, and as a sheep before her shearers is silent, so he did not open his mouth. By oppression and judgment he was taken away. And who can speak of his descendants? For he was cut off from the land of the living; for the transgression of my people he was stricken. He was assigned a grave with the wicked, and with the rich in his death, though he had done no violence, nor was any deceit in his mouth.

Yet it was the LORD'S will to crush him and cause him to suffer, and though the LORD makes his life a guilt offering, he will see his offspring and prolong his days, and the will of the LORD will prosper in his hand. After the suffering of his soul, he will see the light [of life] and be satisfied; by his knowledge my righteous servant will justify many, and he will bear their iniquities. Therefore, I will give him a portion among the great, and he will divide the spoils with the strong, because he poured out his life unto death, and was numbered with the transgressors. He bore the sin of many, and made intercession for the transgressors" (Isaiah 53:1-12).

When it comes to suffering, my question to God is **not**: "Why, God, have You allowed this to happen to me?" but rather, "Why not me?" It's sobering to think of all He did for humankind in spite of the way that He was mistreated and misunderstood while on earth, and even more misunderstood today. Because of the shallowness of our spiritual understanding of who Christ is, we often take our own salvation for granted, and, worse yet, twist it into something that we think we deserve. We often carry our faith in Jesus around like we carry credit cards—we pull it out when we need it. In the meantime, our expectations are not seen through the lens of God, but rather through our own superficial "me-centered" world. Most of us expect to be healthy in body, mind and spirit. I used to expect, and even think that it was due me, to have plenty of clothes to wear and food to eat, a car to drive, a house to live in, a husband who loved me as Christ loves the Church and "perfect" children. I thought this was how life should be, not only for myself, but for everyone. God, however, looks at things a little differently than most of us. He, Who is Sovereign and full of all wisdom has a broader and deeper purpose for our lives. It is profoundly simple: God wants us to love Him, to walk with Him, to learn from Him and to celebrate life in Him. One of the most effective ways God gets our attention and changes our focus is through purposeful suffering.

"And we know that in all things God works for the good of those who love him, who have been called according to his purpose. For those God foreknew he also predestined to be conformed to the likeness of his Son, that he might be the firstborn among many brothers" (Romans 8:28-29).

Our purpose in life is to be conformed to the likeness of His Son, Jesus Christ, not to focus on acquiring worldly possessions. This process of growing into a more mature person happens through God's blessings and through suffering. Both are gifts from God, and, as a result of these things, we are changed to bring Him glory. Christianity is the only religion that sees suffering as a blessing. It is God's tool to allow us to mature in our faith. When we experience suffering, we will be better equipped to know how to comfort others who are going through similar trials. Maybe suffering is not the curse that we have thought it to be. If we draw closer to God, become more sensitive to other's suffering, we are more mature in our understanding of life and death, then we are better for it! In that light, yes, suffering is a blessing.

"Consider it pure joy, my brothers, whenever you face trials of many kinds, because you know that the testing of your faith develops perseverance. Perseverance must finish its work so that you may be mature and complete, not lacking anything" (James 1:2-4).

There is suffering to be expected if we are walking obediently in the footsteps of Christ. Look at what Christ went through. It should not surprise us that a multitude of things go sideways when we are living out the Christian worldview. When those who hate what I am doing with my life are attacking me, it is confirmation that I am doing what God has called me to do, because Satan would not be attacking if I were not following Christ!

"In fact, everyone who wants to live a godly life in Christ Jesus will be persecuted" (2 Timothy 3:12).

There will be a day when there will be no more pain, suffering, persecution or death! (Revelation 21, Isaiah 11, 2 Peter 3). In the meantime, we will all suffer as a result of our own sin, the sin of others, or our sin condition from birth. Know that through it all, there is Jesus, calling us to come to Him so that He can give us the comfort and direction that we need. There is a reason for all of it. Always remember, in the midst of our suffering, there is a God, the great I AM.

I want to share part of a talk that Coach Tony Dungy gave at a breakfast for Athletes in Action before his Super Bowl in 2007. I hope that what Coach Dungy had to say about suffering will help shed some light on this issue and will give you peace as well.

James Dungy, Tony's oldest son, died three days before Christmas. He spoke of the suffering and of what he learned through the experience. "It was tough, and it was very, very painful, but as painful as it was, there were some good things that came out of it." He spoke of how he wished that he had given his son a big hug before he left home for the last time. "I met a guy the next day after the funeral," Tony said. "He said, 'I was there. I heard you talking. I took off work today. I called my son. I told him I was taking him to the movies. We're going to spend some time and go to dinner.' That was a real, real blessing to me."

"We got a letter two weeks ago that two people had received his corneas, and now they can see. That's been a tremendous blessing." Tony also said he received a letter from a girl from the family's church in Tampa. She had known James for many years and went to the funeral. "When I saw what happened at the funeral, and your family, and the celebration and how it was handled, that was the first time I realized there had to be a God. I accepted Christ into my life and my life's been different since that day."

"That was an awesome blessing. So all of those things kind of made me realize what God's love is all about. People asked me, 'How did you recover so quickly?' I'm not totally recovered. I don't know that I ever will be. Because of Christ's Spirit in me, I have the peace of mind in the midst of something that's very, very painful. That's my prayer today, that everyone in this room would know the same thing."

Tony Dungy knows his God and understands the bigger picture of life and suffering. Through his witness, many lives have been changed—including my own.

In the midst of suffering, I AM.

CHAPTER SEVEN

I AM

Chapter 7: I Am

A.W. Tozer, the popular 20th-century author and pastor, asks, "What comes into your mind when you think about God?" He explains, "What comes into our minds when we think about God is the most important thing about us."[1] That's because our understanding of God dictates how we live our lives. If God is not a part of our life, we have no choice but to live by our own convictions, which sometimes include being a wonderful friend and doing service to others. The bottom line is: without God, life does not work. Whether we are aware of it or not, we are all created in God's image, meaning that He designed us to purposely live with Him for His glory. Only then can we live in love, with purpose and with the hope of living forever in Heaven. Knowing God leads to greater devotion, appreciation, honor and gratitude of our relationship with Him.

How can we trust God if we don't know Him? Ask anyone on the street and you will get answers that range from one end of the spectrum to another. "He is good and loving" to "He is vengeful and full of anger." Others say, "He doesn't exist," or "I don't know if He exists." Pantheists would say that god is in everything and everybody. The list of responses is endless. All of these responses cannot be true. Is there **a** God? If so, is it possible to know Him?

The Triunity of God

God wasted no time defining who He is in Genesis 1:1. *"In the beginning God created."* The Hebrew word for God is *Elohim*, a singular masculine noun that is plural in nature. Verse 26 says, *"Then God said, "Let **us** make man in **our** image, after **our** likeness."* Many scholars believe that this is the introduction of the Trinity concept. The word "Trinity" is not used in Scripture, but the notion of the Trinity is found throughout. A few of those references follow: Creation (Genesis 1:1-2; John 1:1-3), Christ's birth (Luke 1:30-35),

Christ's baptism (Matthew 3:16-17) and The Great Commission (Matthew 28:19). The Trinity reflects the perfect and righteous relationship of one being and three persons: the Father, the Son and the Holy Spirit.

According to Dr. James White, author and apologist, "The doctrine of the Trinity is simply that there is one eternal being of God—indivisible and infinite. Three co-equal, co-eternal persons, shares this one being of God: the Father, the Son, and the Spirit.

The three biblical doctrines of the Trinity are as follows:

1. There is one and only one God, eternal, immutable

2. There are three eternal Persons described in Scripture— the Father, the Son, and the Spirit. These Persons are never identified as one in the same—that is, they are clearly differentiated as Persons. (The Father is not the Son, nor is He the Holy Spirit. The Son is not the Father, nor is He the Holy Spirit. The Holy Spirit is not the Son, nor the Father.)

3. The Father, the Son, and the Spirit are identified as being fully deity—that is, the Bible teaches the Deity of Christ and the Deity of the Holy Spirit."[2]

The significance of the Trinity for us can be better understood when we look at this truth: One of the foundational beliefs of Christianity, which sets it apart from all other religious cults and belief systems, is the conviction that Jesus is truly God. In no way does Jesus play a supporting role to the Father and the Holy Spirit. He is fully God just as they are, an equal member of the Trinity. If someone says to you, "I believe in God, but not Jesus," you would know immediately that the person with whom you are speaking is, at best, confused. God is not God without Jesus. God is not God without the Father. And God is not God without the Holy Spirit. God is one being with three separate and distinct persons.

All three persons are equal and in perfect unity with each other, but subordinate in role. God the Father's role is that He has authority over the Son. God the Father is the one who commands, directs and sends. The Son obeys (John 3:16; Romans 8:32; Isaiah 9:6; Galatians 4:4) as does the Holy Spirit (John 14:16 and John 16:7).

Some think that the Holy Spirit is the subordinate member of the Trinity. He, not it, is 100 percent God! He is no less important than the Father or the Son. *"You, however, are controlled not by the sinful nature but by the Spirit, if the Spirit of God lives in you. And if anyone does not have the Spirit of Christ, he does not belong to Christ" (Romans 8:9).*

Because Christ paid the penalty for our sin, we have a restored relationship with Him. God wants to be in a personal relationship with each of us on a moment-by-moment basis, which is why He has given us the gift of the Holy Spirit. Imagine, God living in you! Under the Old Covenant, the Holy Spirit was sent to **be with** those whom the Father had chosen. Now in the New Covenant, the Holy Spirit **lives in**, or indwells, the believer. Upon belief, God sends the Holy Spirit, the Comforter, to dwell in the believer and be a guide for living out their faith in every area of life. No doubt, this is a lifelong process!

"But the Counselor, the Holy Spirit, whom the Father will send in my name, will teach you all things and will remind you of everything I have said to you" (John 14:26). It is through the Holy Spirit that we are daily being transformed into the likeness of God.

"And we, who with unveiled faces all reflect the Lord's glory, are being transformed into his likeness with ever-increasing glory, which comes from the Lord, who is the Spirit" (2 Corinthians 3:18).

The Attributes of God

How do we know who God really is? We know that He cannot be defined by how we feel about Him or by our own life experiences. With complete assurance, we can know who God really is through the Scriptures. God speaks loud and clear for Himself.[3]

God is the One True God. The One True God of the Scriptures is separate from all other gods. He is the One in whom we can put our hope, no longer having to be deceived by the false gods who bring chaos instead of peace into the world. *"I am the LORD, and there is no other; apart from me there is no God. I will strengthen you, though you have not acknowledged me, so that from the rising of the sun to the place of its setting men may know there is none besides me. I am the LORD, and there is no other"* (Isaiah 45:5-6). Because God says He is the One True God, He expects us to worship Him alone. Know, too, that God is the God over all false gods forever. He can never be replaced because He always was and always will be the great I AM (Revelation 22:13).

God Is Good. *"Good and upright is the LORD; therefore he instructs sinners in his ways" (Psalm 25:8).* I can't begin to tell you how many times I have heard someone try to escape the ultimate issue of salvation by saying, "Well, I am a good person. I haven't killed anyone and I volunteer at the Boys Club." My first response to that is, "How do you know you are good enough? Who do you think sets the standard for good?" God is the standard for good; man is not. God is not sometimes good; He is always good because He alone is good. He can never do something bad—it is not in His nature. No one can tag an attribute on God; He is the attribute.

No doubt, you are probably asking yourself, "If God is so good, then why…?" Please refer to our previous chapter: Oh My God. How can a good God allow me to suffer? Suffice it to say that there is much that happens to us, and to others, which makes no sense, but does to God. *"For my thoughts are not your thoughts, neither are your ways my ways, declares the LORD" (Isaiah 55:8).* God is beyond our mind's ability to think or comprehend the reason for suffering. Someday, when we are with Christ in heaven, we will understand. In the meantime, knowing that Scripture is true is essential. Within its pages, we can find comfort in all circumstances, especially those things that we as humans do not understand.

"And we know that in all things God works for the good of those who love him, who have been called according to his purpose" (Romans 8:28). "Peace I leave with you; my peace I give to you. Not as the world gives do I give to you. Let not your hearts be troubled, neither let them be afraid" (John 14:27).

God Is Love. As agnostics when we were planning our wedding, Ed and I decided we wanted to have 1 Corinthians 13 read during the ceremony. It was a part of my sorority ritual and it fulfilled the "requirement" of having some Scripture during the ceremony. It wasn't until years later, as a Christ follower, that I began to understand the significance of these beautiful words. It is through the following verses that God describes Himself. Keep in mind that there is **not** a single one of these attributes of love that comes naturally to us. Yet, they all reflect the heart of God the Father, Son and Holy Spirit. That is why the only way for us to experience any of the attributes of love is for the Holy Spirit to dwell in us and conform us, over time, into His image.

"If I speak in the tongues of men and of angels, but have not love, I am only a resounding gong or a clanging cymbal. If I have the gift of prophecy and can fathom all mysteries and all knowledge, and if I have a faith that can move mountains, but have not love, I am nothing. If I give all I possess to the poor and surrender my body to the flames, but have not love, I gain nothing. Love is patient, love is kind. It does not envy, it does not boast, it is not proud. It is not rude, it is not self-seeking, it is not easily angered, it keeps no record of wrongs. Love does not delight in evil but rejoices with the truth. It always protects, always trusts, always hopes, always perseveres. Love never fails. But where there are prophecies, they will cease; where there are tongues, they will be stilled; where there is knowledge, it will pass away. For we know in part and we prophesy in part, but when perfection comes, the imperfect disappears. When I was a child, I talked like a child, I thought like a child, I reasoned like a child. When I became a man, I put childish ways behind me. Now we see but a poor reflection as in a mirror; then we shall see face to face. Now I know in part; then I shall know fully, even as I am fully known. And now these three remain: faith, hope and love. But the greatest of these is love" (1 Corinthians 13:1-13).

God is love. Not some of the time, not in varying degrees, but fully unconditional love all the time. God could not love you more, no matter what you do or who you are: a believer in Him or not! Whether or not you want to be loved by God, you are. There is nothing you can do to increase God's love for you and nothing you can do to diminish it. He loves you with an ἀγάπη (agape) love that is eternal, pure and unaltered by condition. God loves you because He is love and He created us as the object of His affection—whether we feel like it or not! Therefore, it is impossible to truly love someone unconditionally, perfectly, unless it is God in you (the Holy Spirit) doing the loving. As real as love might feel or seem to be, unless God is in the mix, it is not true, lifelong, or unconditional love.

"Enter his gates with thanksgiving and his courts with praise; give thanks to him and praise his name. For the Lord is good and his love endures forever; his faithfulness continues through all generations" (Psalm 100:4-5).

The things we try to accomplish in the flesh might work for a time, but often do not last. If we decide we want to do something wonderful for God, but He is not the author and sustainer of the event, be assured that He will not receive the glory. Ever wonder why so many "love" relationships do not work? Again, if only God is love and if He is not at the center of a relationship, the girl cannot love the guy as God intended him to be loved, and neither can the guy love the girl as God has designed her to be loved. It's profoundly simple.

Any relationship that is worth something requires work. Find someone who is happily married and ask if a good marriage takes lots of work. No doubt they will smile and agree wholeheartedly. Any friendship takes commitment and time, as does a vibrant relationship with Christ. We get to know Him as we read the Scriptures and pray. Can you imagine how pleased God is when one of His children takes time out of their busy day to sit still, listening to God as He prompts them personally through the Scriptures? The more I am in the Scriptures, the less demanding I am in my own personal requests for fixing things and people, and the more open I become to wanting God's perfect will for my life and the lives of those around me. The Almighty Creator God wants to have a very personal, active, real relationship with us! James 2:23 says, *"And the scripture was fulfilled that says, 'Abraham believed God and it was credited to him as righteousness,' and he was called God's friend."*

God Is Unchanging. Another astounding truth about God is that, unlike us, He never changes. How often do we vary in how we feel toward someone? How many times do we do something that is good one minute, and then turn around and do something that is hurtful the next? God does not have that problem because He is immutable; He never changes. He is who He is.

"Every good and perfect gift comes from above, coming down from the Father of the heavenly lights, who does not change like shifting shadows" (James 1:17).

The good news in this is that God is always good and loving. He can never stop being who He is. Whatever it is that appears to us as God being anything less than good and loving, cannot be true. Because I cannot understand something about God or about some part of Scripture, does not give me the right to assume that God is anything less than good and loving. Since God is unchanging, I know that He will never stop loving or being good to me. This truth gives me much peace as I live each day in a world that is constantly changing.

God Is All Present. From the Scriptures, we learn about the omnipresence of God. He is "all present," which means He is not limited to space or time. God exists everywhere at all times and cannot be contained by anyone or anything.

"'Am I only a God nearby,' declares the LORD, 'and not a God far away? Can anyone hide in secret places so that I cannot see him?' declares the LORD. 'Do I not fill heaven and earth?' declares the LORD" (Jeremiah 23:23-24).

Don't confuse this attribute of God to be pantheistic in nature. The Pantheists believe that God is in everything. The Christian believes that God is separate from His creation, but is present everywhere at all times. There are no random molecules; nothing is beyond God's presence. I remember playing hide and seek with my kids when they were young, and their idea of hiding was to put their hands over their eyes and tell me to try to find them. We laugh, but we probably all did it as we were growing up, because our understanding of life was very limited at that young age. I imagine that God looks upon those who are trying to hide from Him with a bit of a smile on His face as well. There is no secret place from God, either outside or inside your being.

A parent called me before the senior prom night and asked if I would talk to the students about not drinking, not driving fast, not staying out all night and not having sex. As a concerned parent myself, I assured him that I would speak to them. On the Tuesday before prom, at the beginning of class, I told them that I wanted to give them a little advice for the upcoming weekend. It went like this, "I hope that you all have a wonderful time at your proms, and in case you have forgotten, let me remind you of the omnipresence and omniscience of your God, who is all knowing and will always be with you and will never leave your side!" Following moments of awkward silence and a few laughs, we continued with our lesson.

God Is All Knowing. God is also omniscient. Can you imagine a God who knows everything that has ever happened and everything that will ever happen? God is never surprised. *"You know when I sit and when I rise; you perceive my thoughts from afar. You discern my going out and my lying down; you are familiar with all my ways. Before a word is on my tongue you know it completely, O LORD" (Psalm 139:2-4).*

And to think that He loves us anyway!

If I had understood the omniscience of God, I would not have been so surprised to learn about the thousands of prophecies in Scripture that came true hundreds of years after the prophets in the Old Testament had predicted them. That is why I can say with confidence that, when I die, I am going to heaven. Not because I am living a perfect life, because I am not. I know that I am going to heaven because God spoke it in the Scriptures (John 3:16), and because God is the one true God who is always loving, good, true, immutable and all knowing, who would never promise something that He was not going to bring to fruition. This is why Scripture says, *"God is not man, that he should lie, or a son of man, that he should change his mind. Has he said, and will he not do it? Or has he spoken, and will he not fulfill it?" (Numbers 23:19).*

If God knows everything, then why do we pray? When Jesus was in the Garden of Gethsemane, He prayed to the Father about what was about to happen to Him. Jesus knew from the beginning of time that He would suffer a gruesome death on the cross for the sole purpose of paying the penalty for the sins of the world.

"For the wages of sin is death, but the gift of God is eternal life in Christ Jesus our Lord" (Romans 6:23).

He was well aware of what this experience was going to be like, including, for the first and last time from eternity past to eternity future, a momentary separation from the Father. Only when we get to heaven will we ever be able to fully understand the price of the sacrifice Jesus made for all of us on the cross.

Listen to a part of Jesus' prayer: *"He withdrew about a stone's throw beyond them, knelt down and prayed, 'Father, if you are willing, take this cup from me; yet not my will, but yours be done.' An angel from heaven appeared to him and strengthened him. And being in anguish, he prayed more earnestly, and his sweat was like drops of blood falling to the ground" (Luke 22:41-44).*

Do we see it? "Not my will, but Yours be done." Could it be that, when we pray, God wants us to not only praise Him and thank Him for who He is and all that He has done, but also to seek His will, not our own, for our life? Prayer is time for God to make His requests known to us as much, if not more, than it is for us to make ours known to Him. How often do we rip through our checklist, sign off and call it prayer, with no intention of listening to God speak to us through His love letter, the Scriptures?

God Is Faithful. If God knows all about us and sees us at our worst, why does He stick with us? The Bible says that God is faithful, merciful and full of grace. He loves us. That's why, period! God can always be depended on to do what He says. Even when we don't deserve God's love, He is faithful to love us!

"… if we are faithless, he will remain faithful, for he cannot disown himself" (2 Timothy 2:13).

If it were possible to use words to tell of the very nature of God, we would run out of paper and time before the list would be complete. As God is eternal, so are the attributes of His nature. We can talk about His Holiness, His mercy, His righteousness, His truthfulness, His forgiveness, His perfection and His greatness, but even if we take all that is said and written, God and His attributes are beyond our human understanding! He is who He says He is all of the time. Nothing can, or will, change that. We cannot begin to fathom the purity and magnitude of each of the attributes of God with our finite minds.

God, the Father, Son and Holy Spirit is not limited by anything. If He were, He would cease to be God. That is just one thing that separates Him from all other "gods." All other gods are limited in some way, because they are nothing more than man's invention. When we downsize God, we fail to let Him be who He is—the beginning and the end, the Alpha and the Omega.

If we Christians are to promote truth to our culture and live out the Christian worldview with confidence, we have to know who God is, not what our feelings say He may be. God's Word holds the key in giving us a clear picture of the one true God. As we begin to understand who God really is, what is our response? How does it affect our very being? How does it affect the way we live? The more we know of God, the more He can cultivate within us a heart of thankfulness and trust, as well as a willing submission to Him.

Are there areas of our lives we need to give over to God? Are we willing to do it? In submitting completely to His will, we will find greater joy and freedom than we have ever known. We can give up control of our lives, because there is One—the perfect, loving God—who can oversee our lives much better than we ever could. That should come as a great relief to all of us!

Unanswered

CHAPTER EIGHT
I DOUBT IT

Chapter 8: I Doubt It

At this point in our study, you may be thinking, "I get it. I believe in Jesus—I really do. The problem I have is that I still have some doubt about God and my own purpose in life. I simply don't understand some of this stuff. It is gnawing at me, and I don't know what to do with it." There is good news for all doubters: we all doubt! Yes, Christians doubt, and it is OK and even welcomed by God. The things of God can be, and often are, overwhelming mainly because we don't think the way God does and we don't love, live and forgive the way He does either! The key is that the more we get to know God by reading the Scriptures, praying, and reading reliable books that address our questions, the more assured we become of what is true. Truth gives us the peace and the wisdom and the understanding we need to live the way God designed us to each and every day.

What is doubt and from where did it come?

Doubt was first introduced to mankind in the Garden of Eden. It was Satan's goal, then and now, to cause man to take his eyes off of God and worship the created rather than the Creator.

"Now the serpent was more crafty than any of the wild animals the Lord God had made. He said to the woman, 'Did God really say, "You must not eat from any tree in the garden"?'

The woman said to the serpent, 'We may eat fruit from the trees in the garden, but God did say, "You must not eat fruit from the tree that is in the middle of the garden, and you must not touch it, or you will die."'

'You will not surely die,' the serpent said to the woman. 'For God knows that when you eat of it your eyes will be opened, and you will be like God, knowing good and evil.'

When the woman saw that the fruit of the tree was good for food and pleasing to the eye, and also desirable for gaining wisdom, she took some and ate it. She also gave some to her husband, who was with her, and he ate it" (Genesis 3:1-6).

Did you catch it? Doubt was birthed in the first recorded words of Satan: "Did God really say?" Satan was bringing into question the truth of God, His Word and His character. Satan first questioned the truth of God's statement, and then quickly came up against God, contradicting His charge to Eve by offering her something that was appealing and might make her feel good for a time. Because Satan was able to take Eve's heart and mind off of God, she doubted what God had told her and was easily persuaded to disobey Him. Satan added to her doubt by promising her she could be "like God," meaning becoming like God herself. "Satan quickly suggested that man's great desire to be equal to and truly like God, had been deliberately thwarted by divine command. He charged the Creator with selfishness and with a malicious falsehood, representing Him as envious and unwilling for His creatures to have something that would make them like the omniscient One."[1]

The irony about this statement is that it was Satan's own desire to be God that got him in trouble and kicked out of heaven in the first place! (Ezekiel 28:11-19; Isaiah 14:12-20; Luke 10:18) If Eve had believed God and obeyed Him, she never would have bitten on Satan's lie. Eve walked with God and had a relationship with Him. She had it all, but still was looking for something more. Why? Satan knew the weakness of all mankind. He persuaded her, as he continually persuades us to this day, that as great as God is, as much as He loves us, He still withholds from us those things that will make us happy and bring us joy: "Maybe God doesn't want me to be happy. He's a cosmic killjoy. Living for God is nothing more than keeping a bunch of rules—it's keeping me from experiencing the fun the world has to offer." These statements are nothing more than a repackaging of Satan's original lie that deceives us as it did Adam and Eve.

Jesus must have loved teaching the disciples life lessons of what happens when we take our eyes off of Him and trust in our own self-effort. The following example was one they would never forget!

"During the fourth watch of the night Jesus went out to them, walking on the lake. When the disciples saw him walking on the lake, they were terrified. 'It's a ghost,' they said, and cried

out in fear. But Jesus immediately said to them: 'Take courage! It is I. Don't be afraid.' 'Lord, if it's you,' Peter replied, 'tell me to come to you on the water.' 'Come,' he said. Then Peter got down out of the boat, walked on the water and came toward Jesus. But when he saw the wind, he was afraid and, beginning to sink, cried out, 'Lord, save me!' Immediately Jesus reached out his hand and caught him. 'You of little faith,' he said, 'why did you doubt?' And when they climbed into the boat, the wind died down. Then those who were in the boat worshiped him, saying, 'Truly you are the Son of God'" (Matthew 14:25-33).

Peter temporarily took his mind and eyes off of Jesus and immediately began to sink. Sound familiar? When we focus on ourselves by taking our eyes and minds off of Jesus, we, too, begin to sink. We worry and get upset when things do not go our way. We may become quick to judge others or think we are genius at figuring out how to fix something or someone that, only God can restore. All this to say, when we begin to think God is not able to do all things and that He needs us to help, doubt can easily take up residency in our minds and hearts. We can all testify that it does not lead to peace and joy.

Addressing doubt and questions can be overwhelming and complex because emotions often take over. Dealing with unbelief is a process. To be able to claim understanding and victory over most of our doubt takes perseverance and hard work. It is not a quick fix, but those who are willing to allow God to unravel their preconceptions about life, others and God Himself they will become people who have a peace and joy they never knew existed, no matter how good or bad the circumstances.

One kind of doubt is a stubborn doubt that says, "No matter what you say, no matter what evidence says, I choose not to believe in God in any way, shape or form." One who willfully chooses not to believe may be outwardly satisfied, but is not at peace in their state of doubt or unbelief. These people will generally make no effort to find truth that could relieve their doubt, but rather, in their stubbornness, choose to live their lives contrary to God and His Word.

Friedrich Nietzsche said, "Faith means not wanting to know what is true."[2] *"Jesus said to him, 'I am the way, and the truth, and the life. No one comes to the Father except through me' (John 14:6).*

Sadly, for many, they will miss the very thing they are looking for when they turn a deaf ear to God. The stubborn doubter reminds me of what G.K. Chesterton said, "The problem with Christianity is not that it has been tried and found wanting, but that it has been found difficult and left untried."[3]

Be reminded that God is a loving God who is calling all, even the stubborn doubter, to Himself. God will never stop loving or pursuing them. This should alarm the willful skeptic or cynic; God will never force Himself into a person's life, nor will He force anyone to love Him. For those who choose to be stubborn, the door is open for them to change their mind and come to Him. God will not refuse them; He loves those who repent and receive His love and forgiveness. For those who choose to remain closed to God through stubbornness, God has a word for them:

"If any of you lacks wisdom, he should ask God, who gives generously to all without finding fault, and it will be given to him. But when he asks, he must believe and not doubt, because he who doubts is like a wave of the sea, blown and tossed by the wind. That man should not think he will receive anything from the Lord; he is a double-minded man, unstable in all he does" (James 1:5-8).

"So I gave them over to their stubborn hearts to follow their own devices" (Psalm 81:12).

There is nothing healthy or productive about being stubborn and closed to God. For those who have turned away from truth, they have also turned away from life everlasting. Pray for them that God would not harden their hearts to Him, and that, as an act of their will, they would turn to God who is waiting for them!

God loves it when a person who has doubts and questions is not afraid to face them and work through them until they get an answer. These people are reasonable doubters who simply want to know more, but do not know where to go for answers. God encourages us in Scripture to *"test all things and hold on to that which is good" (1 Thessalonians 5:21).*

Most of us have doubts of the mind. For example, we just can't imagine how Jesus could have been brutally beaten and killed on a cross, then put in a tomb with a giant boulder rolled in front of it, and then three days later, poof, there was Jesus walking around. "It makes no sense," we say, "people die and stay dead. It just could not have happened; it must be a fable." However, when one digs into the writings of authors who lived at the time of Christ, the Bible will be found to be true beyond reasonable doubt.

Many have set out to disprove the writings of Scripture and have found that, as a result of their massive research, what was recorded in Scripture was true. One such person was Sir Cecil Wakeley, one of the world's leading scientists whose credentials are rather impressive—K.B.E, C.B., LL.D., M.CH. Doctor of Science, F.R.C.S., and past president of Royal College of Surgeons of Great Britain. He said, "Scripture is quite definite that God created the world, and I for one believe that to be a fact, not fiction. There is no evidence, scientific or otherwise, to support the theory of evolution." Louis Agassiz, a Harvard scientist; Dr. Duane Gish, a biochemist and author; *Michael Faraday*, a physicist who formulated laws of electromagnetic induction and did groundwork for making dynamos, electric motors and transformers; *Samuel F.B. Morse*, who invented the telegraph and from whose name we get Morse code; and *Isaac Newton*, who developed laws of gravity, motion and calculus, are but a few of pioneers in the sciences who strongly supported creation.[4]

There are also doubts of the heart and emotions that cannot be satisfied through reading and studying. These doubts come from those who are deeply suffering; only God Himself can quiet a broken heart. Ravi Zacharias, in his book, *Cries of the Heart,* writes about "a man who had come from a country where much blood had been spilled in internal strife, a land where someone's heart was broken every day by some stray bullet, or a hate-filled ideological conflict. He told me that even though, for years, he had found comfort in the knowledge that Christ had borne his sins, it was new realization, years later, when he took note that Christ had borne our sorrows, too.

That intimacy with God is a knowledge that bridges what one knows with what one feels. Such knowledge takes what we know and what we feel seriously. This is not a fatalistic posture that says, "So be it," resigned to accept what flies in the face of reason. When we learn God's profound answers to every sentiment we feel, we find contentment and courage, and live a life of hope and confidence. We then make every day count with significance, while treasuring His thoughts and harnessing our feelings."[5]

Know that God wants to quiet your heart. No matter who you are, or what you have done or gone through, God is there with you and for you. He wants you to know Him, to learn from Him and to talk to Him. You matter a great deal to God. He died for you, not only to offer you forgiveness for your sins and eternal life, but also so that He might have a relationship with you that is real, life-giving, and full of hope, joy, and peace.

"Here I am! I stand at the door and knock. If anyone hears my voice and opens the door, I will come in and eat with him, and he with me. To him who overcomes, I will give the right to sit with me on my throne, just as I overcame and sat down with my Father on his throne. He who has an ear, let him hear what the Spirit says to the churches" (Revelation 3:20-22).

I want to close this chapter by sharing with you two specific times that God spoke to me about doubts that I had as a new believer. I hope they will encourage you in your spiritual quest.

I was frustrated because nothing made sense to me, so much so that I would often think that God was playing with my mind. He gave me new insight into how He sees things one day when I was in Chicago trying to find my way to the airport. I was driving through the streets with massive buildings on all sides, totally lost. I had no idea how anyone could ever learn to navigate through it. I had to keep pulling over for directions, and finally, by God's grace, I found the airport! The plane lifted off the runway and into the air as we circled around the city, gaining altitude. Suddenly, I saw the city from a distance, and what had seemed impossible to comprehend a few hours earlier became clear. I could see where I had been and where I had to go to reach my destination. I understood for the first time, that much of my own frustration about life and people was because I had such a limited view. I was seeing life from a finite position, and did not and could not see life from God's infinite perspective. For me, it was a turning point in my faith. I needed to be content in what I knew and understood that day, and to be joyful in what God was willing to show me. The more I learned about our infinite and sovereign God, the bigger and more awesome He became to me, and consequently, the more my faith grew and doubts diminished because I could trust Him implicitly to show me where to go when things became confusing.

When I first became a Christ follower, I struggled and doubted my own salvation. I believed that Christ was and is God and that He died for my sins and rose again. What I was not sure of was His acceptance of my faith in Him. My mind was set, but my heart was far away. I was unsure if I would go to heaven when I die. Was I really a Christ follower? Did the Holy Spirit live in me or not? I thought about this all the time, and it was affecting my personal growth in my faith. I sought guidance from a good friend, Anne Walls, who is a wonderful teacher and student of the Scriptures. She told me that Satan was behind this in that he was successfully distracting me from trusting Christ. Her advice was to understand that there are times when we simply must choose to believe, in spite of what our emotions are telling us. She suggested to me that my faith should not just be an emotional response to Christ, but rather, a commitment built on the truth of the Word of God. I needed to fight back my weak faith with Scripture and a truth statement.

From that time on, whenever I got those doubts about my salvation, I quoted John 3:16-17 and said, "Thank You, Lord for making me your child because of my faith in you. Thank you for promising never to leave me. Thank you for assuring me that when I die, I will go to heaven to be with you! Amen." From that moment on, whenever I thought I was not His, I went through my routine. At the beginning, I went through it several times a day. As the days passed, I did it less and less, and within weeks, I no longer had any doubt about my salvation. If you struggle with certain truths about God, try this exercise. You, too, will overcome the doubts of your heart through the work of the Holy Spirit.

Whether it is stubborn, reasonable or heartfelt doubt, God wants to meet us right where we are! He promises that if you look for Him, you will find Him. Where should you look? Your answers will be found in the Scriptures, in prayer and through friends who are wise and living out their faith. Remember that God is faithful and wants you to have true peace and joy. If you seek, you will find. No doubt about it! ✈

CHAPTER NINE
THE "I" OF THE STORM

Chapter 9: The "I" of the Storm

"The material universe is all there is!" says the atheist. "The cosmos is all that there is or all that ever will be," says astrophysicist, Carl Sagan.[1] "We cannot prove that there is no God, but we can safely conclude that He is very, very improbable indeed," writes Richard Dawkins in *The New Humanist*.[2] "Science can teach us, and I think our own hearts can teach us, no longer to look around for imaginary supports, no longer to invent allies in the sky, but rather to look to our own efforts here and below to make this world a fit place to live in, instead of the sort of place that the churches in all these centuries have made it," proclaims Bertrand Russell in *Why I Am Not A Christian*.[3] Voltaire writes, "The truths of religion are never so well understood as by those who have lost their power of reasoning."[4]

All these people have embraced the Humanist (Naturalist) worldview. For the Humanist, reality is one-dimensional. Since there is no belief in God, man cannot think beyond himself or beyond what he has learned in this world to be true. With no belief in God, they believe that no one has a soul. This theory naturally leads to the belief that man is the result of random chance through a biological process of evolution. They espouse that there is no truth beyond science and no morals beyond personal preference.

It is important to remember that our God loves those who do not love Him and continues to pursue and draw all people to Him. Again, we all have the choice to accept or reject Jesus as our Savior; the Naturalist/Humanist has chosen to reject Him. This choice results in taking God out of the equation, leaving man as the center for all truth. Their ideals for success are wealth, status and popularity. The push is for self-actualization, especially through the sciences. In general, the Humanist is the center of his or her own universe, seeking self-rule by pursuing those things that gratify his or her own self-interests.

The ramifications of believing not in God but in man as the center for all truths leads the Humanist into a world philosophy that has no hope, no forgiveness, no purpose greater than themselves and no future beyond this life. Atheistic scientists and pseudointellectuals (those who purport to have all the answers) are attracted to this worldview. With no God, there are no moral absolutes and no value to human life. With no recognition of sin, man bases his value system on his or her personal needs and opinions. As far as questions about life are concerned, the Humanist is free to discover their own answers. The Humanist celebrates reason, even faulty reasoning when it comes to God, values and the origin of life. Humanism emphasizes bringing out the best in people through scientific inquiry, individual freedom, human reason, tolerance and self-determination. They tend to look down on Christianity and see it as a belief system that is of no value and dangerous to all who believe in God.

How does the Naturalism/Humanism worldview answer the "Five Life Questions"?

1. **From where did I come?**

   The universe created itself. The universe (and everything in it) is the result of random, impersonal, undirected forces of nature. We did not come from a transcendent Creator God. Humanity is the result of purposeless evolutionary development over millions of years. In the beginning was the Big Bang.

2. **Why is there such a mess in the world?**

   Man is inherently good, but some people have not fully actualized their human potential. Without this self-actualization, these people do not have the ability to fully cooperate with others.

3. Is there any hope?

Humanity is the only hope for getting the world out of the mess it is in. The pursuit of knowledge and human progress will bring about the eventual elimination of all that is wrong with the world, ultimately making utopia here on earth possible.

4. What is my purpose in life?

Mankind's purpose is to simply pursue mutual agreement and cooperation of basic human wants and needs. All people are to seek the knowledge necessary to fix what's wrong with the world.

5. What happens when I die?

All people will experience a physical death and nothing more beyond this life.

Hopefully, you can see that, although the person who is a humanist may be the nicest person you know—a great community philanthropist, a contributor to the progress in the area of science, a wonderful spouse and parent and friend—they still are separated from God. They have made a conscious decision to reject God and therefore, until they choose to believe in Jesus, they have no hope of going to heaven when they die and no hope of experiencing, in this life, the love, joy and peace that God gives to those whose trust is in Him.

"And this is the testimony: God has given us eternal life, and this life is in his Son. Whoever has the Son has life; whoever does not have the Son of God does not have life" (1 John 5:11-12).

The following is the personal life story of Dr. Jim Williams, who has a tremendous love for God. He has a Ph.D. and works in the anatomy department of a medical university. He has spoken to our Anchorsaway students and his own students through the years on a biblical worldview. I think his story will serve as an encouragement for those wondering how a Humanist thinks and how one might share the love of God with someone like Jim. It's also a story that might stir some thought in someone who is searching for God.

"Growing up, I always loved nature and wanted to be a scientist, so it was natural for me to major in biology in college, and to head off to graduate school after that. Whatever faith in God that I had as a youth evaporated over those years, so that during my post-doctoral research training, I was functionally an atheist, even though I do not remember thinking through much philosophy or religion during that period.

It was shortly after that, in my first faculty position at a college in South Carolina, when my wife said that she wanted to start taking the kids to Sunday school. I remember thinking that it was all pretend, and it wouldn't hurt me to go along just to keep peace in the family. However, I do remember quite a few Sundays when I went to the office, but something happened to me during those times that I did go to church. I began to become intrigued with the Bible; I started reading it every night. I didn't have anyone to talk to about it, and the church that we were in was not very helpful for someone wanting to learn about the Bible. Nonetheless, as the months went by, I grew in hunger for that knowledge.

By the time we moved to Indianapolis, we were dedicated churchgoers, and began looking for a church. We ended up in a Sunday school class that had an excellent Bible teacher. I remember being irritated with him, because he seemed so confident about what he taught. I kept going because, for the first time in my quest for answers, I was in an environment that I felt comfortable in asking questions, as well as learning the material.

That first winter was a great time of change for me. In addition to learning a lot from the Sunday school class, I discovered Christian radio and read a wide variety of Christian books. As the months went by, I had come to see myself as a sinner worthy of hell, who nonetheless, was saved by the sacrifice of Jesus Christ on my behalf. I don't remember much about the process, but it included a lot of study of the Scriptures. I remember being impacted by from the Sermon on the Mount and doing a lot of searching into what the Good News actually means. I soon became a believer in Jesus Christ, and that spring was my first real celebration of Easter, and it was wonderful.

I found myself in a most unusual predicament: I was a professional biologist, doing research in a medical school, and also a follower of Jesus Christ with a growing trust in the Scriptures. It wasn't long until I began to feel the tension between the two.

I started investigating the creation/evolution controversy, and discovered several things right away. First, much of what I had learned as a biology student was not as well supported as I had thought. In brief, the advent of molecular biology in the 1960s has made it harder to imagine how life could have originated from a 'primordial soup,' and it has also made Darwin's theory harder to accept. For example, Darwinian Theory relies on variation among living things. Darwin thought that variation was continuous, so that the steps in the evolution of something (like a wing, or an eye) could happen through a long series of very tiny changes. That is macroevolution. It turns out, though, that living things do not vary in that way. Indeed, even changes in the function of proteins—the building blocks of our bodies—almost always require 'jumps' in protein structure.

To give an example, some proteins are enzymes, like the ones that digest our food. For evolution to change an enzyme into a 'better' enzyme, the process must involve more than just changing the existing enzyme bit by bit, with the change of each little bit making the enzyme slightly better than it was before. You can't improve an enzyme very much by that process. Rather, you need to change the enzyme more dramatically, taking away big chunks of the protein, or adding more big chunks. This is not 'smooth variation,' but rather, 'jumps' in structure. Such jumps in protein structure do not happen by simple variation as Darwin imagined it, and modern evolutionists have not been able to propose ways that this could have happened at the genesis (beginning) of life on our planet.

If you think about the odds of the molecules of life coming into being through a large number of such random events, it would take an irrational leap of faith to believe that life could begin on any planet through random arrangements of molecules. Yet many intelligent people believe exactly that. They trust that the universe is composed only of matter and energy, and put their faith in that, presuming that they must have come into being by a series of chance events.

Of course, it is not just molecules that are unlikely to appear by chance. Molecular biology continues to discover more multi-protein structures and processes that are obvious examples of 'irreducible complexity' (as in Behe's book, Darwin's Black Box). The processes inside of our cells are amazingly complex, with each process requiring multiple steps and multiple proteins, such that it is very hard to imagine how they could have come into being by any sort of unguided genesis. The more science learns about our bodies, the more complex the story gets. Darwin had no idea how complicated living things are, and I suspect that his conclusions would have been very different if he had known the simplest molecular biology!

Despite this, I have seen that my colleagues are largely unable to see these problems as significant. It is as if they are thinking, 'Matter and energy are all there is, so evolution must have happened, even if we don't have a clear idea of how it could have happened.' Frankly, we biologists do not learn enough philosophy in school to see learn how to think about things like this.

Another problem my colleagues have (and I had) is confusing what is called microevolution with macroevolution. Microevolution does, indeed, occur. We can see changes in animals and plants over time, and the scientists who study these things are discovering that some species even set themselves up for change, by carrying out sophisticated swapping of their own DNA, apparently to maximize change over a few generations and enhance the survival of offspring. Changes that have been observed include the alteration of color in moth populations, recovery of lost enzyme functions in bacteria to enable them to resist antibiotics, and changes in beak dimensions in bird populations.

You will see these examples of microevolution used in the newspaper and television to 'prove' that evolution happens. But microevolution does not bring into existence anything new. With microevolution, the moths are still moths, and the bacteria still bacteria.

Macroevolution is the process of new things (wings, eyes) and new creatures coming into being. Such a process has never been seen to occur. Its existence is inferred by evolutionists from fossils and from the similarity in DNA among living things. But fossils could have come from creatures buried in the past (such as in a flood) and DNA similarities among living things can simply indicate that they were created out of the same 'workshop!' As we saw above, life could not have come into being without some outside influence, so there is no need to invoke macroevolution for anything.

Some Christians want to believe in God and evolution, too. We can understand the reasons for this: No one wants to look uneducated in our society, and if you don't believe in macroevolution, you are quickly labeled as foolish and backward in our culture. So, Christians try to put evolution and God together, saying that God created through evolution. The idea of God creating through evolution creates more problems than it solves. If God created through evolution, then death and suffering existed from the beginning of creation, because evolution (both micro and macroevolution) occurs through the death of some, and the survival of others. If death and suffering were part of the creation of life, then most of the Bible has to be thrown out as badly wrong. Indeed, the very idea of Jesus coming to give us 'life' becomes absurd, as the very definition of 'life' is changed.

Christians who embrace evolution end up inventing a God-guided evolution that is very different from what evolutionists believe. And the price of this is a loss of most (if not all) of biblical theology. The stakes of this are high. If you accept evolution, you lose the God of Jesus Christ. I am not stating this too dramatically. For those Christians who struggle with these issues intellectually, I recommend a book by D. Russell Humphreys, *Starlight and Time*.

From the history of science, one can see that, over and over again, scientists were set on a certain way of looking at the universe, only to have that overturned by new theories. We, as Christians, need not fear the discoveries of science. Rather, we must simply wait, and eventually the truth will be known: God created, just as He said."

"For by him all things were created, in heaven and on earth, visible and invisible, whether thrones or dominions or rulers or authorities—all things were created through him and for him. And he is before all things, and in him all things hold together" (Colossians 1:16-17).

"For thus says the LORD, who created the heavens (he is God!), who formed the earth and made it (he established it; he did not create it empty, he formed it to be inhabited!): "I am the LORD, and there is no other" (Isaiah 45:18).

This is not about a personal opinion and it is not about being judgmental, biased or narrow-minded. This is about reality, the truth. This is from the Word of God. The Christian worldview leads to life and the Naturalist/Humanist worldview leads to separation from God, which is death.

With this being true, there is all the more reason for the Christian to become well grounded in what and why they believe in Jesus. Being a former Humanist like Dr. Jim Williams, we are living examples that there is always hope for all people to become a believers in God. I cannot say it enough:

you must be prepared to give an answer to their questions with gentleness and respect. If you are not into science, that is fine. If someone asks you a scientific question and you don't know the answer, find someone who does!

With all this said, the greatest apologetic (defense of the truth of God) is the way you live out your faith. If you know how to defend your faith and speak down to or rudely to someone who does not know what you know, especially in the scientific realm, and make them feel stupid, then you have lost the point of being prepared. However if you are someone who lives out the love of Jesus every day in your home, at work or with friends, and can answer questions with love and respect, then you are speaking God's language!

"You are the light of the world. A town built on a hill cannot be hidden. Neither do people light a lamp and put it under a bowl. Instead they put it on its stand, and it gives light to everyone in the house. In the same way, let your light shine before others, that they may see your good deeds and glorify your Father in heaven" (Matthew 5:14-16).

CHAPTER TEN
A LOVE LETTER

Chapter 10: A Love Letter

We all know that there are a multitude of religious books that claim to have the inside track on God. I found it extremely challenging to figure out which book, if any, is one of absolute truth. Can anyone know, within a reasonable doubt, if the Bible is reliable and inspired by God? The Bible is the foundation of the Christian faith. Is it one that we can trust? Is it true?

I addressed a group of self-proclaimed born again Christian students and asked them this question: "If I were an atheist and asked you to give me a reason for why I should consider reading the Bible, what would you say?" A few hands went up.

"Because it is God's Word!"

"Really?" I said. "How do you know for sure that it is God's Word?"

The once confident student quietly replied, "Because my parents told me so?"

I then asked, "What happens if your parents are wrong? Might there be other parents out there that are telling their children that the Koran is the only religious book that is true? Might there be a good chance that, unless the reliability of the Scriptures can be proven to be the work of God, Christianity is a hoax, and we have all been fools to have studied and followed its teachings?" They became quiet.

Another student, who was convinced that she had solved the question, piped up. "It takes faith to believe that the Bible is true!"

"Faith in what?" I asked her. "Faith in your opinions or feelings?"

"No," she replied, "Just faith."

"It sounds to me that you are saying that in order for me to believe, I would have to commit intellectual suicide, because there is no evidence to prove the truth of the Bible. Is your faith a hunch or a chance, or is it knowing how the Bible was written, what makes it unique, and why man could not, on his own, have written it?" In all my years of teaching and speaking to young adults, I have never, except for my then-8-year-old nephew, Frankie Dame, had anyone give me a solid reason for the hope that they had in the reliability of the Scriptures.

For the Christian, all roads lead to the Bible. If the Bible is true and inspired by God, then everything about the Christian faith can be trusted (Ephesians 3:2-6). If the Bible is authentic, then the following is also true: the Bible is our primary source for learning and understanding life. We can believe the story of creation, the history of Israel, and God's preservation of the Messianic line leading to Christ—all of this is found in the Old Testament. We can also know that the New Testament is the exact account of the fulfillment of all the Messianic prophecies in the Old Testament coming to fruition in the person of Jesus Christ. God ordained the writings in Scripture from the time of Moses to the final writings of the Apostles and Paul in the New Testament, so that we could know Him and understand from where we come, why the world is such a mess, the hope we have in Jesus, our purpose in life, and what happens when we die. It is the single most important apologetic (proof) that the Christian must know in order to communicate truth to others.

If, however, the Bible is merely a collection of stories giving us man's idea of what God might be like, then we are misinformed and should reject all of it. In this world of Postmodernism, many embrace the idea that absolute truth does not exist. (This, by the way, is an absolute in itself!) Today, many churches and Christians embrace this notion as well. As a result, they have a pick and choose mentality when it comes to Scripture, believing some of it, but not all of it. They might believe that God had a role in creation, but did not create. They believe in Jesus as their Savior, but also believe others can be Christians without trusting in Jesus. It is this misdirected theology that has caused much confusion in the Church today.

I grieve for the person who comes to church to learn about God because, like so many others, they know the way they are living is not filling that giant God vacuum in their heart. They go to church because they want to learn truth. Instead they are often fed the worldly philosophy of "just be a good person," or "just be happy," or "give your money and God will heal you and bless you with material wealth." Many so-called seeker-friendly churches have watered down the biblical messages for fear of offending someone and causing tension. However, this tension might be what ultimately ushers many into an authentic relationship with the person of Jesus Christ. For many who are seeking God, they are not learning the truth that changes lives. Because of this, many abandon the hope of knowing God and continue to live out the lie that this life is all there is. Unfortunately, they may have been better off just staying at home and catching up on some sleep. I shudder for those ministers, pastors and teachers who mislead others about the truths of the Scriptures, Jesus, and all mankind. Pastors, speakers and leaders will someday have to give an account to God Himself for the way they lead or mislead their congregation (James 3:1).

The Jews have utmost respect for the Old Testament; they referred to it as God's love letter to them. They see the Scripture as a gift from God that confirms His faithfulness, love and sovereignty. The following paragraphs contain some of what I found in my search to uncover the truth about the Scriptures. I will be forever indebted to Josh McDowell for his extensive research in this area, as reflected in his book, *Evidence That Demands a Verdict*.

Knowing for sure that the Bible is the Word of God is a critical component in building a Christian worldview. The Bible is the foundation for all that we believe to be true about God, the Holy Spirit, and the person of Jesus Christ. Any doubts that we have about our faith or questions others have about Christianity can, and should, be traced back to the Word of God. These truths will not only help you grow in your own faith in God, but will also equip you to always be prepared to give the answer to everyone who asks you the reason for the hope that you have in Jesus Christ, with gentleness and respect (1 Peter 3:15-16).

How do we know it's true? What does God have to say about Scripture? Is God claiming authorship over Scripture?

"All Scripture is God-breathed and is useful for teaching, rebuking, correcting and training in righteousness, so that a man of God may be thoroughly equipped for every good work" (2 Timothy 3:16-17).

"Above all, you must understand that no prophecy of Scripture came about by the prophet's own interpretation. For prophecy never had its origin in the will of man, but men spoke from God as they were carried along by the Holy Spirit" (2 Peter 1:20-21).

Uniqueness of Scripture

As we look into how the Bible was put together, few would disagree that it is the most unique compilation of books ever written. The Bible has been translated into more languages than any other book and is the most widely circulated book in the world, making it the most extensively read and influential book in history. It has survived throughout the ages, despite its intense opposition. The Bible contains a total of 66 books, 39 of them in the Old Testament and 27 in the New Testament. The amazing thing about Scripture is that, throughout all 66 books, there is one theme: the redemption of man through the Messiah, Jesus Christ.

The uniqueness of the Bible is incredible and shows how God wanted to relate and speak to men and women of all ages, professions, cultures, and conditions. Consider that it was written over a time span of 1,500 years, 40 generations, and by 40 different authors from all walks of life. The Bible reflects the different, sometimes extreme, moods of the writers—some wrote from great joy, deep sorrow, and at times, paralyzing fear. It was written on three continents: Asia, Europe, and Africa. It was written in three languages: Hebrew, Aramaic, and Greek. Keep in mind that this was before computers, telephones and jet planes!

These were men writing what the Holy Spirit was prompting them to write, rather than their own collaborative efforts. Would it not have been less cumbersome for God to have just dictated His words through one prophet and have been done with it? Why did He take 1,500 years and all of those people to write it? God could have just made it appear, but He didn't. He chose to use real people from all walks of life, like you and me. They were far from perfect and very different from each other. God wanted the book to be written by a variety of people so that we could relate personally to the writer as they wrote through the inspiration of the Holy Spirit. Over and over again, God chooses the "lowest of these" to do the great things. The same is true today. He has chosen you and me to go, just as we are, into our own culture and be lights, speaking truth into the hearts and minds of those wanting to know truth.

There is so much more to be said about this amazing book. The Bible is so simple, yet so profound, that it can be studied for a lifetime and still not be exhausted. It is also unique in that, unlike cults and other false religions, it is not an account of man's efforts to find God, but rather an account of God's effort to pursue and reveal Himself to man. It contains precisely the things that God wants man to know, in exactly the form that He wants us to know them. What an awesome God we worship!

The amazing uniqueness of the Bible, however fascinating, does not make it true. How then can we prove that the Bible is true?

According to Josh McDowell, there are three ways to prove the reliability of the Bible: the bibliographical test, internal evidence test, and the external evidence test.[1] We will begin with the bibliographical test, which examines the original manuscripts of the Old and New Testaments to determine how they have been handed down to us. This includes the study of the methods that the Jews used to copy the manuscripts, as well as manuscript comparison.

Bibliographical Test: The Scribes

The scribes, meaning counters, followed strict disciplines regarding the writing of the Scriptures. They were the clans of scribes from Jabez, who wrote with meticulous care, insisting on the following conditions that, by today's standards, seem unfathomable:

- The text must be written on the skin of a clean animal.
- Only a Jew could prepare the scroll for use in the synagogue.
- It was fastened together with strings from a clean animal.
- Each skin contained a specified number of columns, equal throughout the entire book.
- The length of each column must extend no less than 48 lines and no more than 60 lines.
- The breadth of each column must consist of exactly 30 letters.
- Each scribe must use a specially prepared recipe of black ink.
- An authentic copy of the text must serve as the example for each scribe to follow.
- The scribes were to copy nothing from memory.
- The space between every consonant could be no more than the width of a thread.
- The breadth between every section must be the same as that of nine consonants.
- Between every book was the width of three lines.
- The Pentateuch must terminate exactly with a line.
- Copyists were required to sit in full Jewish dress.

There was an absolute reverence for Scripture and the name of God, so much so that a fresh quill was used each time the sacred name of God was penned. Nothing could interrupt a scribe while writing God's name, not even the presence of a king! The scribe's job was to produce a master copy because God wanted to make sure His Word was copied accurately.[2]

All this reflects God's desire for us to know the truth and to be set free.

"So Jesus said to the Jews who had believed him, 'If you abide in my word, you are truly my disciples, and you will know the truth, and the truth will set you free'" (John 8:31-32).

Bibliographical Test: Comparison Studies

The second bibliographical test compares the New Testament with accepted books of antiquity. They are compared by the date when each manuscript was written and by the date of the earliest copy. The shorter the time span between these two dates would mean a more accurate copy. Also, a greater number of manuscript copies allows for a better manuscript testimony. What is the comparison between the New Testament and other ancient historical writings?

Many of us have read the writings of Caesar, Plato, Socrates and Aristotle and believed them to be accurate as written. Let's take a closer look.

Plato wrote between 427-347 BC, with the earliest copy dating from AD 900. This means the time span between the original and the first copy was 1,200 years, with only seven surviving copies.

Aristotle wrote between 384-332 BC, with the earliest copy dating from AD 1100. This leaves a time span of 1,400 years between the original and the first copy, with only 49 copies.

Of all the ancient Greek and Latin literature, Homer's Iliad, as a work of antiquity, possesses the greatest amount of manuscript testimony. It was written in 900 BC, with the earliest copy dating from 400 BC, a time span of 500 years, with 643 copies.

When we compare the New Testament with these ancient texts, we find that it was written between 40-100 AD, with the earliest copy dating from 125 AD—a span of only 25 years from the original. In addition, the New Testament copies number more than 24,000.

The evidence is astounding! When we put this together with the uniqueness of the Bible and how it was written, it passes the bibliographical test with flying colors. There is no other book like it!

Historian J. Harold Greenlee rightfully concludes, "Since scholars accept as generally trustworthy the writings of the ancient classics even though the earliest MSS (handwritten copies of the Scriptures) written so long after the original writings and the number of extant MSS is in many instances so small, it is clear that the reliability of the text of the New Testament is likewise assured."[3]

In the next chapter we will examine the internal evidence, external evidence, and how all these writings were put together to become the Word of God! ✈

CHAPTER ELEVEN
SCIENCE & NUMBERS

Chapter 11: Science & Numbers

The Bible is both unique and accurate in its transmission of text, but it is also perfect in prophecy, amazing in archeological support, and was confirmed by Jewish historical writers of the day. No other religious book can come close to such claims. All this proves beyond a shadow of a doubt that all of Christianity is verifiable. Proof is not a matter of someone's bias; it is the truth. In this chapter we are going to look at the prophecies, archeological finds, the words from writers of antiquity about what happened during the time of Christ.

Internal Evidence Test: Prophecy

In my search to find whether or not Christianity was true, the revelation of fulfilled prophecies became a giant anchor for my growing faith in Christ. If every prophecy in the Scriptures is true, then the Book would have had to be inspired by God Himself. With the Bible being the only holy book of antiquity that has significant prophecies, all having been fulfilled except for those that are recorded as future events, it has clearly set itself considerably apart from other religious writings. "Specific prophecies are conspicuously absent from the 26 other religious books that claim to be scripture, including the Muslims' Koran, the Book of Mormon, the Hindu Vedas, and Buddhist writings.[1] If there were one prophecy that stands out from all the other 2000, it would be the one in Psalm 22 claiming Christ would be crucified. What makes this so amazing is that the prophecy was written before there were crucifixions. You will see this prophecy and many more as you read on.

God's thumbprint is all over His Word. Take the time to read it carefully and examine the facts. I think that you will conclude, as I did, that it takes much more faith **not** to believe in God's inspiration of the Bible than it does to believe in it.

In all of Scripture, there are more than 2,000 prophecies with approximately 333 of them that point to the Messiah.

Of those 333, there are 48 prophecies that do not overlap one another; these are called "pure prophecies." The question for this section is: What are the odds of one man fulfilling all 48 prophecies?

Peter Stoner, in *Science Speaks,* studied the probability of one man fulfilling just eight prophecies as listed below:

1. BORN AT BETHLEHEM

Prophecy: "But as for you, Bethlehem Ephrathah, too little to be among the clans of Judah, from you One will go forth for Me to be ruler in Israel. His goings forth are from long ago, from the days of eternity" (Micah 5:2, NAS). 750 BC

Fulfillment: Jesus was born in Bethlehem of Judea (Matthew 2:1; John 7:42).

2. PRECEDED BY MESSENGER

Prophecy: A voice is calling, "Clear the way for the Lord in the wilderness; Make smooth in the desert a highway for our God" (Isaiah 40:3; Malachi 3:1, NAS). 433 BC

Fulfillment: John the Baptist came, preaching in the wilderness of Judea, saying, "Repent, for the kingdom of heaven is at hand" (Matthew 3:1-3, 11:9-10; Luke 1:17; John 1:23, NAS).

3. HE WAS TO ENTER JERUSALEM ON A DONKEY

Prophecy: "Rejoice greatly, O Daughter of Zion! Shout in triumph, O daughter of Jerusalem! Behold, your king is coming to you; He is just and endowed with salvation, humble, and mounted on a donkey, even on a colt, the foal of a donkey" (Zechariah 9:9, NAS). 520 BC

Fulfillment: "And they brought it to Jesus, and they threw their garments on the colt, and put Jesus on it. And as He was going, they were spreading their garments in the road" (Matthew 21:6-11; Luke 19:35-36, NAS).

4. BETRAYED BY A FRIEND

Prophecy: "Even my close friend in whom I trusted, who ate my bread has lifted up his heel against me" (Psalm 41:9, 55:12-14, NAS). 300 BC

Fulfillment: Judas Iscariot was the one who betrayed Him (Matthew 10:4, 26:49-50, NAS).

5. SOLD FOR 30 PIECES OF SILVER

Prophecy: "And I said to them, 'If it is good in your sight, give me my wages; but if not, never mind!' So they weighed out thirty shekels of silver as my wages" (Zechariah 11:12, NAS). 520 BC

Fulfillment: Judas Iscariot asked the price of betrayal, and "they weighed out to him thirty pieces of silver" (Matthew 26:15, 27:3, NAS).

6. MONEY TO BE THROWN IN GOD'S HOUSE

Prophecy: "So I took the thirty shekels of silver and threw them to the potter in the house of the Lord" (Zechariah 11:13b, NAS). 520 BC

Fulfillment: "And he threw the pieces of silver into the sanctuary and departed" (Matthew 27:5a, NAS). "And they counseled together and with the money bought the Potter's field as a burial place for strangers" (Matthew 27:7, NAS).

7. DUMB BEFORE ACCUSERS

Prophecy: "He was oppressed and He was afflicted, yet He did not open His mouth" (Isaiah 53:7, NAS). 700 BC

Fulfillment: "And while He was being accused by the chief priests and elders, He made no answer" (Matthew 27:12, NAS).

8. HANDS AND FEET PIERCED

Prophecy: They pierced my hands and my feet (Psalm 22:16; Isaiah 53:5, NAS). 520 BC

Fulfillment: "And when they came to the place called the Skull, there they crucified Him" (Luke 23:33, NAS).

Peter Stoner states, "We find that the chance that any man might have lived down to the present time and fulfilled all eight prophecies is 1 in 10^{17} (or 1 in 100,000,000,000,000,000). Let us try to visualize this…Suppose we take 10^{17} silver dollars and lay them on the face of Texas. They will cover all of the state two feet deep. Now, mark one of these silver dollars and stir the whole mass thoroughly, all over the state. Blindfold a man and tell him that he can travel as far as he wishes, but he must pick up one silver dollar and say that this is the right one. What chance would he have of getting the right one? Just the same chance that the prophets would have had of writing these eight prophecies and having them all come true in any one man, from their day to the present time, providing they wrote them in their own wisdom."[2]

When Stoner considers 48 prophecies, he says, "We find the chance that any one man fulfilled all 48 prophecies to be 1 in 10^{157}." For anyone to fulfill all 48 biblical prophecies is scientifically absurd.

Chuck Missler has also studied the probabilities of one man (Jesus) fulfilling all 48 Old Testament prophecies.[3] Missler says that the probability of one man fulfilling 16 of the 48 prophecies is 1 in 10^{45}. His concept model is a ball of silver dollars with a radius 30 times the distance of the Earth to the Sun. He follows the same idea as Peter Stoner's illustration of the Texas concept model. He also accepts the probability of all 48 prophecies being fulfilled in one man as being one in 10^{157}. There is no concept model for this, because this number is bigger than the human mind can begin to grasp. Thumbprint of God? You decide. One can choose to reject Jesus Christ as the Son of God, but if so, keep in mind that he or she is rejecting a fact proven more absolutely than any other fact in the history of mankind.

Internal Evidence: Archaeology

God could have stopped the chain of evidence confirming the reliability of the Scripture with the fulfillment of prophecy, but He didn't! The Bible has served as a major tool in the hands of archaeologists as their findings verify cities, king, prophets, nations and a multitude of artifacts confirming the existence of biblical history. The Green family, founders of Hobby Lobby, has the largest private collection of more than 40,000 biblical texts and artifacts. Without evidence, the Bible could, and should, be written off as myths or stories. Archeological findings are in the thousands, including, but certainly not limited to, the Dead Sea Scrolls, the house of David inscription, amulet scroll, the Ebla tablets, a Galilean boat, and a Pontius Pilate inscription proving the existence of what was previously discounted. "It may be stated categorically that no archeological discovery has ever controverted a single biblical reference. Scores of archeological findings have been made which confirm in clear outline or in exact detail historical statements in the Bible"[4]

God, however, continues to shout to a deaf world the truth of the Word and the truth of His own existence in a multitude of arenas. There is more internal evidence as we look into the science of archaeology. In what ways have the discoveries of archaeology verified the reliability of the Bible? Over the years there have been many criticisms leveled against the Bible concerning its historical reliability. These criticisms are based on a lack of evidence and often time, personal bias. Since the Bible is a religious book, many scholars take the position that it cannot be trusted, unless it has corroborating evidence from extra-biblical sources. In other words, the Bible is guilty until proven innocent, and a lack of outside evidence places the biblical account in doubt.

This standard for reliability is far different from that applied to other ancient documents, even though many, if not most, have a religious element. They are considered to be accurate, unless there is evidence to show that they are not. Although it is not possible to verify every incident in the Bible, the discoveries of archaeology since the mid-1800s have demonstrated the reliability and plausibility of the Bible narrative.

I had a student contact me to say that his professor had said the Bible was not a reliable book of antiquity, because there was no alphabet at the time of Moses. The student's faith was shaken. Yearly, there are new claims by atheists who try to undermine the reliability of the Scriptures. On the surface, they seem to know what they are talking about but always upon further investigation, atheists are found to be, at best, misinformed. Was there an alphabet in the time of Moses? Yes! The discovery of the Ebla archive in northern Syria in the 1970s has shown the biblical writings concerning the Patriarchs to be viable. Documents written on clay tablets dating from around 2300 BC demonstrate that personal and place names in the Patriarchal accounts are genuine. The name "Canaan" was in use in Ebla, a name critics once said was not used at that time and was written incorrectly in the early chapters of the Bible. The word *tehom* ("the deep") in Genesis 1:2 was said to be a late word demonstrating the late writing of the creation story. *Tehom* was part of the vocabulary at Ebla, in use some 800 years before Moses. Ancient customs reflected in the stories of the Patriarchs have also been found in clay tablets from Nuzi (Northern Iraq) and Mari (Mesopotamia).

"When compared against secular accounts of history, the Bible always demonstrates amazing superiority. The noted biblical scholar R.D. Wilson, who was fluent in 45 ancient languages and dialects, meticulously analyzed 29 kings from 10 different nations, each of which had corroborating archeological artifacts. Each king was mentioned in the Bible as well as documented by secular historians, thus offering a means of comparison. Wilson showed that the names as recorded in the Bible matched the artifacts perfectly, down to the last jot and tittle! The Bible was also completely accurate in its chronological order of the kings. On the other hand,

Wilson showed that the secular accounts were often inaccurate and unreliable. Famous historians such as the Librarian of Alexandria, Ptolemy, and Herodotus failed to document the names correctly, almost always misspelling their names. In many cases the names were barely recognizable when compared to its respective artifact or monument, and sometimes required other evidence to extrapolate the reference."[5]

External Evidence

Our final proof for testing the reliability of the Bible comes from the examination of literature separate from the Bible that confirms its accuracy. The historical writers during the time period in question were not believers in Jesus Christ; they were men merely reporting what they knew to be true. As contemporary, outside sources, these writings also confirm the reliability of Scripture.

Eusebius of Caesarea (AD 263-339)—His Ecclesiastical History preserved the writings of Papias, bishop of Hieropolis (AD130). Papias, a friend of the Apostle John, wrote: "The Elder (Apostle John) used to say this also: Mark, having been the interpreter of Peter, wrote down accurately all that he (Peter) mentioned, whether sayings or doings of Christ, not, however, in order. For he was neither a hearer nor companion of the Lord; but afterwards, as I said, he accompanied Peter, who adapted his teachings as necessity required, not as though he were making compilation of the sayings of the Lord. So then Mark made no mistake, writing down in this way some things as he (Peter) mentioned them; for he paid attention to this one thing, not to omit anything that he had heard, nor to include any false statement among them."[6]

Flavius Josephus (AD 37-100?)—As a Jewish historian, he wrote one of the most comprehensive histories of the Jewish people, primarily for the benefit of the non-Jewish world. In The Antiquities of the Jews, he wrote: "Now there was about this time Jesus, a wise man, (if it be lawful to call him a man,) for he was a doer of wonderful works, a teacher of such men as receive the truth with pleasure. He drew over to him both many of the Jews, and many of the Gentiles. (He was the Christ) and when Pilate, at the suggestion of the principal men amongst us, had condemned him to the cross, those that loved him at the first did not forsake him, (for he appeared to them alive again the third day) as the divine prophets had foretold these and ten thousand other wonderful things concerning him; and the tribe of Christians, so named from him, are not extinct to this day."[7]

The Bible is an amazing collection of books, inspired by God and recorded by man. He wanted us to know beyond a shadow of a doubt that the words were inspired by Him. We saw this confirmed through the different tests of reliability for books of antiquity: bibliographical, internal, and external tests. We looked at the way it was written, the comparison with other works, the prophecies, and multiple examples of how archaeology supports the biblical account. Can there be any doubt that the Creator of this vast universe and all that is in it is also the author of the greatest Book ever written? It is a work of love from the Creator to us.

We can learn much about the nature of God as we study the evidence of the trustworthiness of this book of antiquity. God cares that we know the truth.

"Jesus answered, 'I am the way and the truth and the life. No one comes to the Father except through me. If you really knew me, you would know my Father as well. From now on, you do know him and have seen him'" (John 14:6-7).

Perhaps the best way to summarize the Bible is to say that God invites each one of us to read, study and learn the Scriptures so that we can live out those truths that are found within its covers. It is our instruction manual for living life to its fullest and for impacting our culture for Christ.

Unanswered

CHAPTER TWELVE
NOT WHAT I EXPECTED

Chapter 12: Not What I Expected

Have you ever noticed how easy it is to talk about God, but speaking openly about Jesus is taboo? If you are looking for a great way to ruin a discussion at work, in school or in a social gathering, just talk about Jesus. Why is that so? Might it be that "god" is a generic term referring to whatever anyone wants it to mean, making it a "safe" word to use? Jesus, there is something about that name! The very mention of Jesus often narrows the field as people become very emotional about what they think concerning this man who is called the Savior.

In Mark 8:27, Jesus questioned his disciples, asking them, *"Who do people say I am?"* The answers they gave Him were as varied as they are today. Our world is saturated with a variety of ideas about Jesus stemming from many different worldviews. There are some, as taught by Mormon doctrine, which embrace the radical notion that Jesus was the brother of Lucifer, while others believe He was just a prophet. Many say He was a great moral teacher and philosopher, "a wonderful wise man, nothing more." Still others suggest He was the greatest human being to ever walk the earth. Many call Jesus God in human form. All religions can't be right.

Who is this Jesus? This is the fundamental question that each of us must answer if we are to ever know true salvation. The Christian worldview, in contrast to all other religions and belief systems, is built on the belief that Jesus Christ was more than a good teacher, a prophet, or wise sage. He is both God and sinless man, and His deity has and continues to have an overwhelming impact on mankind.

In Christianity, the Old and New Testaments are consistent in their portrayal of Christ's deity. This may surprise you, but Jesus is called: Creator (John 1:3, Colossians 1:15-17, Hebrews 1:10), Lord of Lords and King of Kings (Revelation 17:14, 19:16, 1 Timothy 6:14-16), Savior (Acts 2:21, 4:12, Romans 10:9), Rock (1 Corinthians 10:4, Isaiah 8:14), The First and the Last (Revelation 1:17, 2:8, 22:13), Judge (2 Timothy 4:1, 2 Corinthians 5:10, Romans 14:10) and I AM (John 8:24, 58,

13:19, 18:5). So many of these terms are often thought to be reserved for God the Father, but are also manifested in Christ, Himself. What does all of this mean? Jesus is God!

What specifically do other religions have to say about Jesus? In Hinduism and Buddhism there is no recognition given to Christ. Rabbinic Jews believe that there are two Messiahs: one is the Son of Joseph who would die, and the other is the Son of David, who would establish His kingdom on earth. The Koran is presently the only holy book of the Muslim religion. One of their holy books used to be the Injil, which is the New Testament, but the Muslim will tell you that it is corrupted and Jesus is not their Savior, but only a prophet of God. Hinduism, Buddhism, Islam and all cults believe that their salvation comes through some form of works. "How much work must I do to know and be accepted by God?" you might ask. The answer? "You just keep working!"

I remember a camping trip that our family took up into Maine. We had our van packed to the brim with enough gear to spend weeks in the wilderness. Our kids were all young teenagers and were lukewarm, as was their mother, about the whole camping idea. None of us had a voice in the decision but Ed, being an Eagle Scout, thought it would be great for us to experience nature firsthand. In the evening by the campfire, there were bets from Scott, Mark and Andrew as to who would wimp out and end up sleeping in the van. All claimed to be courageous and tough. We closed down camp, Ed told one of his scary stories and the boys settled down in their tents. Kelly made no such claims of bravery and insisted on sleeping with me in the van. In the morning I woke up, and to my surprise, the fearless ones were sound asleep throughout the van. The only one left in his tent was Ed!

Anyone can make a claim. We might claim to be tough and unafraid, but no mere human can be that all the time in all situations. There was only one man who made a claim that only God could make—that was Jesus. Jesus claimed to be God, the I AM. Jesus also said that He would be killed, buried, and rise again in three days. If He could do this, and He did, then Jesus Christ is truly God.

The Christian writer, C.S. Lewis, explains the significance of Christ's claims to deity: "…Among these Jews there suddenly turns up a man who goes about talking as if He was God. He claims to forgive sins. He says He has always existed. He says He is coming to judge the world at the end of time. Now let us get this clear. Among Pantheists, like the Indians, anyone might say that he was a part of God, or one with God: there would be nothing very odd about it. But this man, since He was a Jew, could not mean that kind of God. God in their language meant the Being outside the world Who had made it and was infinitely different from anything else. And when you have grasped that, you will see that what this man said was, quite simply, the most shocking thing that has ever been uttered by human lips…I am trying here to prevent anyone saying the really foolish thing that people often say about Him: 'I'm ready to accept Jesus as a great moral teacher, but I don't accept His claim to be God.' That is the one thing we must not say. A man who was merely a man and said the sort of things Jesus said, would not be a great moral teacher. He would either be a lunatic—on a level with the man who says he is a poached egg—or else he should be the Devil of Hell. You must make your choice. Either this man was, and is, the Son of God: or else a madman or something worse. You can shut Him up for a fool, you can spit at Him and kill Him as a demon; or you can fall at His feet and call Him Lord and God. But let us not come with any patronizing nonsense about His being a great human teacher. He has not left that open to us. He did not intend to."[1]

In the Garden of Eden (Genesis 3), Adam and Eve chose to disobey God. The penalty was a physical death (we will all die) and a spiritual death, which is separation from having fellowship with God. Adam and Eve had to leave the garden, because God did not want them to eat from the tree of eternal life in their newfound fallen state. God wanted to restore them from their sin. In Genesis 3:15, God promised that there would be a Messiah who would come and pay the penalty for their sins, re-establishing an intimate relationship with Him, through the indwelling of the Holy Spirit, with all who believed. Jesus Christ would prove His deity; He would pay once and for all the penalty of sin for all mankind by willingly going to the cross, dying, and three days later, coming to life again! That is the Gospel—the good news!

The resurrection of Jesus Christ is the focal point of the Christian faith. It is recorded in Scripture as being the single most important event in the history of mankind and was the culmination of Christ's life on earth. The apostle Paul believed it to be true and wrote about it.

"Now, brothers, I want to remind you of the gospel I preached to you, which you received and on which you have taken your stand. By this gospel you are saved, if you hold firmly to the word I preached to you. Otherwise, you have believed in vain. For what I received I passed on to you as of first importance: that Christ died for our sins according to the Scriptures, that he was buried, that he was raised on the third day according to the Scriptures, and that he appeared to Peter, and then to the Twelve. After that, he appeared to more than five hundred of the brothers at the same time, most of whom are still living, though some have fallen asleep. Then he appeared to James, then to all the apostles, and last of all he appeared to me also, as to one abnormally born" (1 Corinthians 15:1-8).

Did the resurrection really happen?

"But if it is preached that Christ has been raised from the dead, how can some of you say that there is no resurrection of the dead? If there is no resurrection of the dead, then not even Christ has been raised. And if Christ has not been raised, our preaching is useless and so is your faith.... If only for this life we have hope in Christ, we are to be pitied more than all men" (1 Corinthians 15:12-13,19).

Strong words from the inspired Apostle Paul—if Christ did not rise from the dead, then Christianity is a complete hoax and those who believe it are to be pitied. However, if it did happen, then the Bible, history and the historians would all support this amazing event. Do they?

As we study the death and resurrection of Christ, be assured that this was no surprise to Christ. He knew that He would die for the sins of the world. He knew the costs, which we can only imagine, and He even talked about it with His disciples.

"'We are going up to Jerusalem,' he said, 'and the Son of Man will be betrayed to the chief priests and teachers of the law. They will condemn him to death and will hand him over to the Gentiles, who will mock him and spit on him, flog him and kill him. Three days later he will rise'" (Mark 10:33-34).

What was it about Jesus that caused the Jews to be in such an uproar that they would want to kill Him? Scripture again gives us the answer. Jesus asked the people for which miracle they were stoning Him.

"'We are not stoning you for any of these [miracles],' replied the Jews, 'but for blasphemy, because you, a mere man, claim to be God'" (John 10:33).

We can also see that Jesus had such compassion, not only for the disciples, but also for those who were yet to be born. In the midst of His personal agony, Jesus was praying for all of us as He was in the Garden of Gethsemane.

"My prayer is not for them alone. I pray also for those who will believe in me through their message, that all of them may be one, Father, just as you are in me and I am in you. May they also be in us so that the world may believe that you have sent me. I have given them the glory that you gave me, that they may be one as we are one: I in them and you in me. May they be brought to complete unity to let the world know that you sent me and have loved them even as you have loved me. Father, I want those you have given me to be with me where I am, and to see my glory, the glory you have given me because you loved me before the creation of the world. Righteous Father, though the world does not know you, I know you, and they know that you have sent me. I have made you known to them, and will continue to make you known in order that the love you have for me may be in them and that I myself may be in them" (John 17:20-26).

What a beautiful, loving, tenderhearted, and courageous God we worship! If you have time, go back and feast on the whole chapter of John 17 to learn more about the heart of our Lord.

Jesus finished praying and soon Judas, one of Jesus' best friends, came into the garden. Jesus even had Judas sitting at his right side, the place of honor, during the Last Supper. He loved Judas; I am sure that the heart of Jesus was breaking because He knew that Judas had rejected the love Christ had offered to him. More than disbelief, He had betrayed the Son of God. How it must break the heart of God, when He looks into the hearts of those whom He created who have also turned away from His love.

It was dark in the garden, but Jesus most likely heard the battalion of men coming up the hill, and saw the reflective light of the torches as they came into the garden to arrest Him. They were coming to arrest God!

In the midst of the chaos, Jesus was still showing His deity and loving His own, as well as those who wanted to kill Him.

"Jesus, knowing all that was going to happen to him, went out and asked them, 'Who is it you want?' 'Jesus of Nazareth,' they replied. 'I am he,' Jesus said. (And Judas the traitor was standing there with them.) When Jesus said, 'I am he,' they drew back and fell to the ground" (John 18:4-6).

Picture it. All who knew Jesus knew that He did not carry weapons and had never fought anyone. Nevertheless, into the garden marched close to a hundred fully armed soldiers, along with the "religious" leaders. What happened when Jesus merely spoke His name? They all fell down! Can you imagine what that must have looked like? They picked themselves up off the ground and, once again, asked Jesus who He was. He again confirmed that He was Jesus of Nazareth and then asked that His friends be released.

"Then Simon Peter, who had a sword, drew it and struck the high priest's servant, cutting off his right ear. (The servant's name was Malchus.) Jesus commanded Peter, 'Put your sword away! Shall I not drink the cup the Father has given me?'" (John 18:10-11).

I really don't blame Peter. Even though Jesus had specifically told Peter what must happen to Him in Jerusalem, because Peter loved Jesus as his Lord and friend, he tried to defend Him. Cutting off Malchus' ear gave Jesus another opportunity to show His deity.

"When Jesus' followers saw what was going to happen, they said, 'Lord, should we strike with our swords?' And one of them struck the servant of the high priest, cutting off his right ear. But

Jesus answered, 'No more of this!' And he touched the man's ear and healed him" (Luke 22:49-51).

Jesus touched the man's ear and he was healed. This healed soldier is the same man who fell over upon hearing the name of Jesus, and now he was receiving a miracle of healing! One would think that the soldier would have, right then, bowed down to worship Jesus as God! What about Judas? He was there also and most likely was one who also fell down hearing Jesus say His name. We can only imagine the terror that ripped through them when they came to the realization that Jesus is the healer, the Son of God. Isn't it amazing how our biased presuppositions can blind us when we are faced with truth? I am reminded to pray for those in my life who have done the same thing: heard the truth of Jesus, but have not ingested it because of their own stubbornness. I pray that the hearts and minds of all those who are too obstinate to hear or see the truth would be opened by God.

After Jesus revealed His deity to the soldiers, they bound and arrested Him. It was Friday, and there continued to be many accusations against Christ. He went through six trials, three Roman and three Jewish. Jesus then stood before the governor, Pilate, and made a personal appeal about who He was and His purpose for being on earth (John 18:37-40). Have you ever known people who asked a question, but really didn't want to know the answer? Pilate asked Jesus a question about truth, but immediately walked out to the crowds of people and asked what they wanted him to do with Jesus. It seems that Pilate found more comfort in a crowd of people than he did with God. The people wanted Jesus crucified and Pilate was going to give them the desire of their heart. Trying to play both sides of the fence, Pilate said that he did not think that He was deserving of death, but that he would permit it. Jesus says in Matthew 12:30, *"He who is not with me is against me…"* Sitting on the fence when it comes to Jesus is not an option. With the decision made to kill Jesus, Pilate sent Him to be whipped.

"They stripped him and put a scarlet robe on him, and then twisted together a crown of thorns and set it on his head They put

a staff in his right hand and knelt in front of him and mocked him. 'Hail, king of the Jews!' they said. They spit on him, and took the staff and struck him on the head again and again. After they had mocked him, they took off the robe and put his own clothes on him. Then they led him away to crucify him" (Matthew 27:28-31).

It was customary to tie the accused to a post at the tribunal. The criminal was stripped of his clothes, and severely whipped by the lictors, or scourgers. For those who have seen Mel Gibson's movie, *The Passion of the Christ,* you will no doubt remember the scene. The Pharisees wanted the Romans to crucify Jesus, because the Pharisees were limited to 40 lashes. There were no limitations for the Romans. The whip, known as a flagrum, had a sturdy handle that connected to leather strips of varying lengths. Sharp jagged pieces of bone and lead were woven into them. It was expected for the prisoner to be whipped to the point that the skin was shredded off the severely bruised body, with just enough blood left to get him to the cross.

Once on the cross, the soldiers nailed Jesus' wrists and feet to the cross. He was only two or three feet above the ground, and was at a place where all those coming to celebrate Passover would walk by Him, spit on Him or hurl insults at Him. Thousands of Jews were coming into the city for Passover, a tradition to celebrate God's mercy that He showed the Jewish nation, and there, right in the midst of the Roman and Jewish crucifixion, hung God!

He was given some wine vinegar to drink by someone standing near. Everyone then said, *"Now leave him alone. Let's see if Elijah comes to save him." Jesus* then cried out and *"gave up his spirit" (Matthew 27:49-50).*

Friday evening came (until the resurrection of Christ, the Jewish Christ followers worshiped on Saturday), and Joseph of Arimathea asked for the body. Pilate double-checked to make sure that the body of Jesus was dead, and then, and only then, did he release it to Jesus' friend, Joseph (Mark 15:42-45). Joseph, together with Nicodemus, took Jesus' body and prepared it for burial according to the Jewish customs (John 19:39-40).

Aromatic spices, composed of fragments of fragrant wood pounded into a dust known as aloes, were mixed with a gummy substance known as myrrh. Starting at the feet, they would wrap the body with the linen cloth. Spices mixed with the gummy substance were placed between the folds. They would wrap to the armpits, put the arm down, and then wrap to the neck. A separate piece was wrapped around the head. The entire encasement weighed between 117 and 120 pounds. When the wrappings around Christ dried out, they resembled a cocoon.

The prepared body of Christ was placed in a new tomb, hewn out of solid rock, in a private burial area. Jewish tombs usually had an entrance 4 ½ to 5 feet high. Most tombs, or sepulchers, of this period had a forecourt that led into the burial chamber. A rectangular pit in the center of the burial chamber enabled one to stand upright. Around the chamber were a number of couches upon which the body was placed. Early sepulchers had a groove, or trough, cut into the rock in front of them to hold the stone that sealed them. The trough was designed in such a way that its lowest part lay immediately in front of the entrance. When the block holding back the stone was removed, the stone would roll down and lodge itself in front of the opening. The tomb was sealed shut with the official authority and signet of Rome.

Remember at the beginning of this chapter, you read how Jesus told His disciples what was going to happen to Him? It happened just as He said it would. So Pilate sent out another Roman guard to guard the tomb. (I wonder if Malchus was in that group.) The Romans knew what Jesus had said and had to make sure that no one stole the body of Jesus and then claimed that He had risen from the dead. This would have been a great threat to Pilate and his rule over his kingdom. Little did he know that God's Kingdom was about to make quite an entrance!

A Roman guard unit was a 4-to-16-man security force. Each man was trained to protect six feet of ground. The 16 men in a square of four on each side were supposed to be able to protect 36 yards against an entire battalion and hold it. Normally, what they did was this: four men were placed immediately in front of what they were to protect. The other 12 were asleep in a semi-circle in front of them with their heads pointing toward the middle. In order to steal what these guards were protecting, thieves would first have to walk over those who were asleep and then get past those who were awake. Every four hours, another unit of four was awakened, and those who had been awake went to sleep.

Fast-forward to Sunday morning when Mary Magdalene, along with other women, went to the tomb early while it was still dark (John 20:1). The boulder had not just been moved away, it had been *airo*, which is the Greek word that means, "to pick something up and carry it away."[2] Had the disciples wanted to steal the body of Jesus, they would have had to tip-toe around the sleeping guards and then roll the 1½-to-2-ton rock up a slope away from the entire massive sepulcher, to such a position that it looked like someone had picked it up and carried it away. Those soldiers would have heard and seen that stone being moved. They would never have allowed that to happen. If a prisoner escaped under the watch of Roman soldiers, the penalty was to be burned at the stake!

"...some of the guards went into the city and reported to the chief priests everything that had happened. When the chief priests had met with the elders and devised a plan, they gave the soldiers a large sum of money, telling them, 'You are to say, "His disciples came during the night and stole him away while we were asleep." If this report gets to the governor, we will satisfy him and keep you out of trouble.' So the soldiers took the money and did as they were instructed. And this story has been widely circulated among the Jews to this very day" (Matthew 28:11-15).

It appears that the soldiers and the Jewish officials were a bit confused. If the soldiers were sleeping, how could they say the disciples stole the body? Either they were asleep or awake; if they were awake, why would they allow the body to be taken away? If asleep, how could they know that the disciples took it away? The Jews' argument does not dispute that the tomb was empty; it gives an alternate explanation of why it was empty. This is a feeble attempt to stamp out the new Christian movement and also illustrates how desperate they were to do so.

There were no guards numerous enough, rock big enough, or wounds deep enough to keep Jesus in the tomb. After she saw the empty tomb, Mary left to report the news of Jesus' missing body to Peter and John.

"So Peter and the other disciple started for the tomb. Both were running, but the other disciple outran Peter and reached the tomb first. He bent over and looked in at the strips of linen lying there but did not go in. Then Simon Peter, who was behind him, arrived and went into the tomb. He saw the strips of linen lying there, as well as the burial cloth that had been around Jesus' head. The cloth was folded up by itself, separate from the linen. Finally the other disciple, who had reached the tomb first, also went inside. He saw and believed. (They still did not understand from Scripture that Jesus had to rise from the dead.)" (John 20:3-9).

It is not hard to imagine the sight that greeted the eyes of the apostles when they reached the tomb: the stone slab, the collapsed grave clothes, the shell of the head-cloth and the gap between the two. No wonder they "saw and believed." A glance at these grave clothes proved the reality of the resurrection. They were like a discarded chrysalis, or cocoon, from which the butterfly had emerged.

"Then the disciples went back to where they were staying. Now Mary stood outside the tomb crying. As she wept, she bent over to look into the tomb and saw two angels in white, seated where Jesus' body had been, one at the head and the other at the foot. They asked her, 'Woman, why are you crying?' 'They have taken my Lord away,' she said, 'and I don't know where they have put him.' At this, she turned around and saw Jesus standing there, but she did not realize that it was Jesus. He asked her, 'Woman, why are you crying? Who is it you are looking for?' Thinking he was the gardener, she said, 'Sir, if you have carried him away, tell me where you have put him, and I will get him.' Jesus said to her, 'Mary.' She turned toward him and cried out in Aramaic, 'Rabboni!' (which means 'Teacher'). Jesus said, 'Do not hold on to me, for I have not yet ascended to the Father. Go instead to my brothers

and tell them, 'I am ascending to my Father and your Father, to my God and your God.' Mary Magdalene went to the disciples with the news: 'I have seen the Lord!' And she told them that he had said these things to her" (John 20:10-18).

According to Jewish principles of legal evidence, women were invalid. They did not have a right to give testimony in a court of law. Therefore, if the resurrection accounts had been manufactured, women would never have been included in the story, at least, not as first witnesses. Christ loves men and women alike, and shows no bias to either one, unlike the Jewish law. Isn't it just like Jesus to let the women to be the first to spread the good news, "He has risen?"

Christ's appearances were not only confirmed by the women, but by many others. *"For what I received I passed on to you as of first importance: that Christ died for our sins according to the Scriptures, that he was buried, that he was raised on the third day according to the Scriptures, and that he appeared to Peter, and then to the Twelve. After that, he appeared to more than five hundred of the brothers at the same time, most of whom are still living, though some have fallen asleep. Then he appeared to James, then to all the apostles, and last of all he appeared to me also, as to one abnormally born" (1 Corinthians 15:3-8).*

Paul says in effect, "If you don't believe me, you can ask them." When the disciples of Jesus proclaimed the resurrection, they did so as eyewitnesses, and they did so while people were still alive who had contact with the events about which they spoke. In 56 AD, Paul wrote that more than 500 people had seen the risen Jesus and that most of them were still alive (1 Corinthians 15:6). As Thomas Hale points out, "If Jesus had, in fact, not risen from the dead, Paul could not have written these words; there were too many people still around who would have called him a liar!"[3]

It passes the bounds of credibility that the early Christians could have manufactured such a tale, and then preached it among those who might easily have refuted it simply by producing the body of Jesus.

The transformation of the disciples speaks louder than the written evidence as to the truth of the resurrection of

Christ. Now, to all who believe, the Holy Spirit, God Himself, would live in their hearts. Because of this, the disciples were transformed into courageous men who later died as martyrs. They never would have done such a thing if it were a deliberate fabrication. They were willing to face arrest, imprisonment, beating and horrible deaths. Not one of them ever denied the Lord or recanted his belief that Christ had indeed risen. This is unparalleled in history.

Scripture has told the story, history supports it, and historians have written more on this subject than on any other historical event in history. Professor Thomas Arnold, author of the three-volume *History of Rome*, and an appointee to the chair of modern history at Oxford University, writes: "I know of no one fact in the history of mankind which is proved by better and fuller evidence of every sort, to the understanding of a fair inquirer, than the great sign which God had given us that Christ died and rose again from the dead."[4]

Author, Dr. D. James Kennedy in his book, *Why I Believe,* wrote: "The evidence for the resurrection of Jesus Christ has been examined more carefully than the evidence for any other fact in history. It has been weighed and considered by the greatest of scholars, among them Simon Greenleaf, the Royal professor of law at Harvard from 1833 to 1848 who helped bring Harvard Law School to preeminence and who has been called the greatest authority on legal evidences in the history of the world. When Greenleaf turned his mind upon the resurrection of Christ and focused upon it the light of all the laws of evidence, he concluded that the resurrection of Christ was a reality, that it was a historical event, and that anyone who examined the evidence for it honestly would be convinced this was the case."[5]

The truth of the death and resurrection of Christ is another anchor for our soul that will hold us secure in the very worst storms of life. Life circumstances often cause us to be disappointed, discouraged and detached from others. Knowing that Jesus is alive and that He is our hope is all that we will ever need. To know that He loves and cares for us enough to endure the cross must serve as a comfort to our souls.

Because Jesus died for the sins of the world, He is the Savior. Why Jesus instead of some person or animal as a sacrifice for our sins? The answer is because He is Holy and without sin, and therefore, He alone is qualified to be the Redeemer for all of humanity. God required a perfect sacrifice to satisfy a perfect, sinless God. When Jesus died on the cross, the penalty for our sins was paid in full. Because of His sacrifice, we are righteous (blameless) in the eyes of a Holy God. It's not because of anything we did, but because of what God did for us! Our relationship is made right with God when we accept and believe that He died for us.

The fact that Jesus was more than just a man, that He was truly God, should give us a sobering appreciation for the sacrifices He willingly made so that we might be saved. Our salvation means that God first comes to us; man does not have to invent a way to find Him. Nor do we have to earn our way to heaven; salvation is God's gift of grace to those who are willing to accept it. And when we do trust Jesus as our Lord and Savior, God promises we will live with Him forever. What a deal!

By hearing the whole story of the resurrection, there should be no doubt in our minds that God loves us, and proved it through the whole experience of the cross. What difference does the death and resurrection of Jesus make in our life in this very moment? If He can love those who whipped Him, drove nails into His flesh, spit and yelled obscenities at Him, then, my friend, He can and does love you right where you are right now. You are free to be who He created you to be and you don't have to worry about making sure your good works outweigh the bad. When you believe in Jesus as your Savior, you are forgiven. You never have to spend a minute separated from the Creator of the universe because the same power that brought Christ back to life is the same power that is working in you today!

Now who do you say He is? ✈

Unanswered

CHAPTER THIRTEEN
NO FREE LUNCH

Chapter 13: No Free Lunch

When you think about the God of the Old Testament, do you see a God who is relational, loving, personal, faithful, kind and forgiving? Probably not. Instead, many of us think of the Old Testament God as being distant, judgmental and angry. In this chapter, not only are we going to see if such ideas about God are true, but we are also going to look at the bigger picture of God's nature and His redemptive plan for all of us. To do this, we are diving into the book of Genesis to study what happened between God and Abraham that shaped mankind's destiny. Through the lens of the Abrahamic covenant we will discover that not only is God consistent in His character throughout the entire Bible, but that He is a God of unmerited love and grace.

Covenant making can be traced back to nearly every culture since the dawn of history. The concept of a covenant is still widespread among many nations of the world. However, the more civilized a society becomes, the more it tends to shy away from the primitive nature of covenants. Covenant models like commitment, faithfulness, loyalty, everlasting, and unconditional love tend to scare us. Instead, today in our culture we hear the words: "keep your options open; if it feels good, do it; nothing lasts forever; I want to renegotiate; no strings attached." Our sophisticated society is simply more prone to embracing the ink of a contract rather than the blood of a covenant. Contracts are more convenient, more independent, and offer more wiggle-room.

The covenant between Abram and God was a Suzerain vassal covenant which, by definition, is an unconditional covenant initiated by a person/tribe/nation vastly superior in power and authority to another party. It was graciously imposed for the lesser one's good. Some of the covenant elements included a representative from each party who spoke and acted on others' behalf and served as a guarantor of the covenant. Specific responsibilities of the covenant were laid out and a blood sacrifice of an animal was required. Both parties would also cut their own arm until it bled and would leave a scar. After the cutting, a vow was taken: "I will keep this covenant even if my own blood has to be shed. If I break this covenant then my own blood will be shed." The parties exchanged pledges to be true to the covenant, shared a meal (Genesis 26:28-31) and a memorial (Genesis 26:32-33).

The words of a covenant reflect an action that is taken as a result of the covenant being made—we see these words throughout all of Scripture. They include: loving kindness, loyalty or faithfulness, mercy, unfailing or steadfast love, peace, friendship, compassion, remembrances, oaths, blessings and curses. Covenant is what holds God's grand narrative together!

The Abrahamic covenant shows God's love toward Abraham and his seed (you and me) and reveals His faithfulness in fulfilling His promise by willfully sacrificing Himself in payment for the sins of ALL mankind. When you read Genesis 15 and see that Abraham—and all men and women who follow—are saved by grace and not performance, you will be amazed. For me, studying the Abrahamic covenant put an end, once and for all, to my struggle with trying to earn and sustain God's love and acceptance.

Genesis 15:1 opens with a vision that Abram/Abraham received from God. It was unusual because Abram had never before received one. Notice the kindness of God as He addresses Abram. *"Fear not, Abram, I am your shield; your reward shall be very great."* In Genesis 12, God had promised heirs, a great nation, and possession of the Promised Land. Abram knew God well enough to question Him. "How can I know?" he asked. God wanted to make sure that Abram would understand the seriousness of this moment, so He decided to cut a covenant with Abram through an animal ceremony. Abram must have been familiar with this as he responded to God's command by knowing what to do with the animals.

"So the Lord said to him, 'Bring me a heifer, a goat and a ram, each three years old, along with a dove and a young pigeon.' Abram brought all these to him, cut them in two and arranged the halves opposite each other; the birds, however, he did not

cut in half. Then birds of prey came down on the carcasses, but Abram drove them away" (Genesis 15:9-11).

Historically, the animals were cut in two pieces and placed opposite each other with the blood from the animals gathering in a trough-like path dug in the ground. Dr. Ray Vanderlaan, historian and master teacher, writes, "The two parties—the greater party who establishes the terms of the covenant first, and the lesser party who either accepts or rejects the terms second—then walked through the blood as a way of saying, 'May what was done to these animals be done to me if I do not keep this covenant.' The one who failed to keep the covenant paid for it with his life.

It's no wonder a *'thick and dreadful darkness'* comes over Abram (v.12). Abram has found himself in the middle of a blood path ceremony with Almighty God. As the sun sets, Abram is looking at all this blood, possibly still unsure as to what his terms are going to be in the covenant, and he's terrified. Maybe God has already told Abram what he expects from him. When the covenant is reaffirmed and circumcision added in Genesis 17, it's clear that God demands Abram to *'walk before me and be blameless'* (17:1). If that is Abram's responsibility in the agreement at this stage, it is evident why he is frightened. A horror of great darkness falls on him. At that moment, God takes all the responsibilities and the burden for fulfilling the covenant upon Himself.

As Abram looks on in a petrified trance of terror, God appears in the darkness as a smoking fire pot. Abram knows it is God and the author of Genesis assumes his readers also know because the greater party always walks through the blood first and the smoke always represents the presence of the Lord. The picture is crystal clear to God's people. The Lord loves Abram so much that He promises to give him a son, descendants, land, and eventually, through Him, the Messiah to save the world. He symbolically tramples barefoot through the blood to give Abram assurance and confidence that he can trust the word of the Lord. God doesn't rebuke or otherwise chastise Abram for questioning Him or for asking for a sign. He just gives Abram what he needs in the form of a common, yet deadly serious, ritual."[1]

We can only imagine what Abram was thinking. It was now his turn to walk the blood path signifying that he would have happen to him what happened to the animals should his side of the covenant not be fulfilled. Terror was overwhelming him because he knew he sinned and he knew that he could not hold up his part of the covenant. Then, because God so loved Abram, He walked the blood path in Abram's place as shown by a blazing torch, also representing God. The torch passes through the pieces down the blood path. The conditions from Genesis 17 apply not only if Abram sins, but also if any of his descendant's sin. God, then, did to Himself what was done to the animals to pay the price for Abraham's sin and for the sins of all of us who were yet to be born. That was the death sentence for His Son, Jesus.

Some 1,700 years later, Jesus Christ, according to the will of the Father, willfully gave His life to pay the penalty for the sin of all: past, present and future. *"For God so loved the world that He gave his only son, that whoever believes in Him shall not perish but have everlasting life" (John 3:16).*

What can we learn from the Abrahamic covenant? God can be trusted to be faithful to His promises. God offers the gift of salvation by the way of the cross without man doing anything. God's grace and plan from the beginning of time, through the Old and into the New Testament, could not be stopped. God pursues us and wants to bless us. And God is good.

My good friend, Pastor Rob Price, opened my eyes to the beautiful story of a covenant love between David and King Saul's son, Jonathan. After David had killed the Philistine, he was brought to King Saul for a talk. It must have been a discussion long enough for David to tell King Saul and his son Jonathan of His faith in the Lord, which no doubt resonated with Jonathan. At that moment, Jonathan loved David as much as he loved himself, even when it was clear that David would succeed King Saul as king. *"And Jonathan made a covenant with David because he loved him as himself. Jonathan took off the robe he was wearing and gave it to David, along with his tunic, and even his sword, his bow and his belt"*

(1 Samuel 18:3-4). David lived and worked for Saul and was very successful in all that he did. People hailed David as a greater warrior than Saul, who became enraged with jealousy and attempted to have David killed several times.

David and Jonathan finalized the covenant terms: *"May the Lord be with you as he has been with my father. But show me unfailing kindness like the Lord's kindness as long as I live, so that I may not be killed, and do not ever cut off your kindness from my family—not even when the Lord has cut off every one of David's enemies from the face of the earth. So Jonathan made a covenant with the house of David, saying, 'May the Lord call David's enemies to account.' And Jonathan had David reaffirm his oath out of love for him, because he loved him as he loved himself"* (1 Samuel 20:13-17).

After many battles, Saul and his sons, including Jonathan, were killed in battle. With the king dead, the royal family and all the staff had to flee the palace out of fear of the enemy killing them as well. *"Jonathan, son of Saul, had a son who was lame in both feet. He was five years old when the news about Saul and Jonathan came from Jezreel. His nurse picked him up and fled, but as she hurried to leave, he fell and became disabled. His name was Mephibosheth"* (1 Samuel 31, 2 Samuel 4:4). They all went to live in Lo-Debar.

Mephibosheth was most likely raised to fear and intensely dislike David. David had taken over the throne, and most of Mephibosheth's family was killed. He was forced to live in hiding, hoping that David would not come and kill all of them. Then, years later, King David remembers his covenant with Jonathan. He had promised to take care of Jonathan's family. David asked his servant if there was anyone left in Jonathan's family to whom he could show kindness. The servant said that there was a young son of Jonathan's named Mephibosheth. King David ordered his men to find him and bring him to the palace. David's men tracked down Mephibosheth and obeyed the king's orders (2 Samuel 9).

Mephibosheth faces David and is told of a covenant made between the king and his own father Jonathan before he was born. Mephibosheth must decide his own fate: choose to enter into the covenant protection, blessings, promises and peace or else be executed as both a terrorist and a covenant-breaker! Mephibosheth declared himself conquered, not by weapons, but by a covenant of love. Mephibosheth realized he was included in a covenant before he was even born! It took years for Mephibosheth to fully change his way of thinking toward life and toward David, but at the end of his life he embraced this amazing covenant (2 Samuel 9).

There is something about covenant love that is both overwhelming and comforting. By studying it, I am reminded again how serious God is, beyond our human understanding, about His love, protection, and provision for His children. His grace is not to be taken lightly. We deserve nothing. What more could He do for us? When He says He loves you, He means it, has proven it, and you can believe it because it is true.

What should be our response to the realization of what He did for us? For me, it makes me want to ask for nothing, but offer up praise and thanksgiving to Him for who He is and for all He has given to me and those who believe. I want to ask forgiveness for not thoroughly appreciating Him and loving Him back by the way I think, speak, walk and pray.

God made a covenant of love with Jesus for our sake, even before we were born. Once we are made aware of that covenant, we have a choice to make: to either come into that covenant relationship or to reject it. If we choose to be a part of that covenant relationship, we are given the opportunity to enjoy the blessings, promises, and peace of God for all of eternity. If, however, we reject that covenant, spiritual death, separation from God, awaits us.

CHAPTER FOURTEEN
FORWARDING ADDRESS

Chapter 14: Forwarding Address

Have you ever watched a movie about someone who needs extreme protection? As the plot thickens, the only solution to the predicament is to send the person in danger away and change his identity. In the process, the victim has to learn who they are and adapt to a whole new way of living. This often involves learning a new language, studying a new culture, adjusting to new schedules, and through time, learning a new way of thinking and processing. Perhaps you, like me, can relate this to the time you made a conscious decision to choose to believe in Jesus as your Lord and Savior. Although we did not immediately know what had happened to us, our identity was now one of God's completely forgiven children. He wasted no time in lavishing His grace on us, but in our newness of being God's child, the reality of what happened and who we have become is at times overwhelming. It is impossible to comprehend all that God has done for those who believe. *"Yet to all who received him, to those who believed in his name, he gave the right to become children of God..."* *(John 1:12).*

For new and long-time Christ followers alike, it is good revisit those days when you first believed. Hopefully, we can see God's faithfulness in maturing us and giving us a deeper understanding of whom we have become and how great our God is! We often forget the miracle of salvation that God offers to all Christ followers. No question about it, when we became believers, God and his angels rejoiced! *"Just so, I tell you, there is joy before the angels of God over one sinner who repents"* *(Luke 15:10).* The Greek word for repent is metanoia, which means "a change of mind." Over time, as we begin to live for someone other than ourselves, we start to not only see ourselves differently, but also our lives, our family, and, most importantly, God. My own perspective of God changed from a God of denial to a God who loves to lavish gifts on us.

Ephesians is a wonderful book in Scripture in which Paul makes it very clear to Whom we belong. He also emphasizes the gifts of grace that God has bestowed on all who believe. It is like Christmas on steroids! *"**Grace** to you and **peace** from God our Father and the Lord Jesus Christ. Blessed be the God and Father of our Lord Jesus Christ, who has **blessed us in Christ with every spiritual blessing** in the heavenly places, even as he **chose us in him** before the foundation of the world, that we should be **holy and blameless** before him. **In love he predestined us for adoption** as sons through Jesus Christ, according to the purpose of his will, to the praise of his **glorious grace**, with which **he has blessed us in the Beloved.** In him we have **redemption through his blood, the forgiveness of our trespasses,** according to the **riches of his grace,** which he **lavished upon us, in all wisdom and insight making known to us the mystery of his will,** according to his purpose, which he set forth in Christ as a plan for the fullness of time, to **unite all things in him, things in heaven and things on earth.** In him we have **obtained an inheritance,** having **been predestined according to the purpose of him who works all things according to the counsel of his will,** so that we who were the first to hope in Christ might be to the praise of his glory. In him you also, when you heard the word of truth, the gospel of your salvation, and believed in him, were **sealed with the promised Holy Spirit, who is the guarantee of our inheritance** until we acquire possession of it, to the praise of his glory" (Ephesians 1:2-14).*

Volumes could be written about the blessings God has given to those who place their trust in Him. One of the most amazing gifts God has granted us is the gift of adoption into His family—we are His children through Jesus Christ, which was His will. Paul's use of the word adoption *(huiothesia),* means a son into the divine family. "Adoption was a well-known legal procedure in the Greco-Roman world. Several Roman emperors during Paul's life used adoption as the means of choosing a successor when they had no legal heir. Adoption guaranteed a number of privileges: (1) The adopted son become[s] the true son . . . of his adopter . . . (2) The adopter agrees to bring up the child properly and to provide the necessities of food and clothing. (3) The adopter cannot repudiate his adopted son. (4) The child cannot be reduced to slavery. (5) The child's natural parents have no right to reclaim him. (6) The adoption establishes the right to inherit."[1]

God chooses His words carefully. Adoption is a word that not only identifies our eternal relationship with God, but also His faithfulness to all of His children. It guarantees that we belong to God and God alone. No one can take us out of His hand. Our Abba Father promises that, through adoption, He will bring us up and provide for us. That is why He has blessed all of His children with the gift of the Holy Spirit, who, at the moment of belief, takes up residence in us.

"I am going to send you what my Father has promised; but stay in the city until you have been clothed with power from on high" (Luke 24:49).

"And if anyone does not have the Spirit of Christ, he does not belong to Christ" (Romans 8:9b).

Christ kept His word and gave what He promised—the Holy Spirit. We learn through the New Testament that, among other things, the Spirit gives life (John 6:63), empowers (1 Samuel 16:13; Matthew 3:16, Acts 1:8), protects (Ephesians 6:17), cleanses us (1 John 1:9), convicts us of sin (John 16:8-11) and guides us through all of life (Matthew 4:1; Luke 4:1).

The number of Christians who believe that Jesus died for their sins, but still do not believe that they are completely forgiven from all past, present and future sins is astronomical. We all know that we are far from perfect and do not deserve the sinless Christ giving up His life to save ours. But He did! That kind of forgiveness and sacrifice goes way beyond our human understanding. For most of us, we forgive (for the most part), but rarely forget. From our own selfish perspective, we are left wondering if Christ's death on the cross could accomplish such a thing. It just doesn't seem fair. But, God made a covenant with Abraham that He would die for the sin of the world and, because He is true to His word, He did just that! Christ hung on the cross and said before He died, "It is finished." He was talking about the payment for the penalty of all humanity's sin that was settled by His death on the cross. It was over. Finished! Christ paid it for all because He loves us and wants us to be free from the penalty of sin, which is spiritual death, separation from Him. He wants us to focus on more important things: Loving God and others outrageously!

We are all broken people who are in desperate need of re-assurance that we can come before God forgiven and washed clean of our sin. Our forgiveness has absolutely nothing to do with how we feel or what we have done in the past, but rather on the truth of God's Word. The following verses should give you great comfort about the depth of God's love for you and forgiveness for your sins.

"...Jesus said, 'It is finished.' With that, he bowed his head and gave up his spirit" (John 19:30).

"But now that you have been set free from sin and have become slaves to God, the benefit you reap leads to holiness and the result is eternal life" (Romans 6:22).

"Therefore, there is now no condemnation for those who are in Christ Jesus, because through Christ Jesus the law of the Spirit of life set me free from the law of sin and death" (Romans 8:1-2).

"Blessed is he whose transgressions are forgiven, whose sins are covered. Blessed is the man whose sin the Lord does not count against him and in whose spirit is no deceit" (Psalm 32:1-2).

"Let us then with confidence draw near to the throne of grace, that we may receive grace and find mercy in time of need" (Hebrews 4:16).

As we begin to think of the impact the cross has on each of our lives, it is important to know what God's expectations are for us. God has commanded us to love Him, to obey Him and to love others. He has, through His covenant love, truly made us one of His! Here are some of the descriptions in the New Testament that illustrate who we are as Christ followers: I am the salt of the earth (Matthew 5:13). I am the light of the world (Matthew 5:14). I am a child of God (John 1:12). I am part of the true vine, a channel of Christ's life (John 15:1, 5). I am Christ's friend (John 15:15). I am chosen and appointed by Christ to bear His fruit (John 15:16). I am a joint heir with Christ, sharing His inheritance with Him (Romans

8:17). I am a new creation (2 Corinthians 5:17). I am God's workmanship, His handiwork, born anew in Christ to do His work (Ephesians 2:10). I am righteous and holy (Ephesians 4:24). I am a citizen of heaven, seated in heaven right now (Philippians 3:20; Ephesians 2:6). I am hidden with Christ in God (Colossians 3:3). I am chosen of God, holy and dearly loved (Colossians 3:12; 1 Thessalonians 1:4). I am a son of light and not of darkness (1 Thessalonians 5:5). I am one of God's living stones, being built up in Christ as a spiritual house (1 Peter 2:5). I am NOT the great "I am" (Exodus 3:14; John 3:28, 8:58), but by the grace of God, I am what I am (1 Corinthians 15:10).

What is our response to all of this? When we consider all that Christ has done for us, how can we keep from loving Him, from wanting to serve Him and be used by Him to bring others into His family? If we believed all of this to be true, we would! If only…

Questions we may have with all this are: What happens when I mess up? What happens when I make mistakes and act out in my old pattern of self-centeredness? What happens when I knowingly go against God and hurt others in the process?

The root of the problem is that we struggle to see ourselves the way God sees us. With our new identity in Christ we understand, to some degree, that belief in Christ changes everything about who we are and our relationship with God. We also know that our hearts, thoughts, and actions are not immediately in sync with our new selves. We all struggle with messing up. This is common among Christians young and old, and the apostle Paul, the primary writer of the New Testament, was no exception.

"For I do not understand my own actions. For I do not do what I want, but I do the very thing I hate. Now if I do what I do not want, I agree with the law, that it is good. So now it is no longer I who do it, but sin that dwells within me. For I know that nothing good dwells in me, that is, in my flesh. For I have the desire to do what is right, but not the ability to carry it out. For I do not do the good I want, but the evil I do not want is

what I keep on doing…For I delight in the law of God, in my inner being, but I see in my members another law waging war against the law of my mind and making me captive to the law of sin that dwells in my members. Wretched man that I am! Who will deliver me from this body of death? Thanks be to God through Jesus Christ our Lord!" (Romans 7:15-20, 22-25).

Paul found victory over this duplicity in his life, not through his own hard work, but through the power of Jesus Christ. The power that God put into us through the Holy Spirit allows us to choose to not cave into our old selfish ways of doing things. We can, as God's children, choose whether we are going to live for God's glory or our own. Sin no longer has power over us!

"We know that our old self was crucified with him in order that the body of sin might be brought to nothing, so that we would no longer be enslaved to sin. For one who has died has been set free from sin. Now if we have died with Christ, we believe that we will also live with Him. We know that Christ, being raised from the dead, will never die again; death no longer has dominion over him. For the death he died he died to sin, once for all, but the life he lives he lives to God. So you also must consider yourselves dead to sin and alive to God in Christ Jesus. Let not sin therefore reign in your mortal body, to make you obey its passions. Do not present your members to sin as instruments for unrighteousness, but present yourselves to God as those who have been brought from death to life, and your members to God as instruments for righteousness. For sin will have no dominion over you, since you are not under law but under grace" (Romans 6:6-14).

The old self is who we were before our conversion to Jesus Christ. Sometimes it is helpful to see who we were when we had no choice but to act out in a godless fashion.

"The heart is deceitful above all things, and desperately sick; who can understand it? I the LORD search the heart and test the mind, to give every man according to his ways, according to the fruit of his deeds" (Jeremiah 17:9-10).

"For from within, out of the heart of man, come evil thoughts, sexual immorality, theft, murder, adultery, coveting,

wickedness, deceit, sensuality, envy, slander, pride, foolishness. All these evil things come from within, and they defile a person" (Mark 7:21-23).

"But now the righteousness of God has been manifested apart from the law, although the Law and the Prophets bear witness to it—the righteousness of God through faith in Jesus Christ for all who believe. For there is no distinction: for all have sinned and fall short of the glory of God, and are justified by his grace as a gift, through the redemption that is in Christ Jesus..." (Romans 3:21-24).

"For the wages of sin is death, but the free gift of God is eternal life in Christ Jesus our Lord" (Romans 6:23).

Now, as a new person in Christ, we are no longer filled with those things that are of the flesh. We have a new heart that is nurtured and strengthened through studying the Word and through prayer. Like all new things, we have to consciously choose to live by our new identity. If we continue to walk closely with God, our life will, day by day, conform more to the image of Christ. We must pray, sometimes moment by moment, that God would destroy the old voice in us that tells us that we do not matter to God, that we are not loved, and that God will never use us to further His Kingdom. Those are lies that we must consciously dismiss, filling that void with truth from the Word of God. That is why spending time in the Bible is critical for our personal growth in Christ.

As a new believer, I was not sure if this new life of mine was going to be fun and exciting or full of boredom mixed with drudgery. I came into this faith loving life, and I sure did not want to give up being with friends, family, or playing golf. I was convinced that God had to have some secret agenda that would keep me from being me and loving life. I am not the religious type and was not about to fake a more serious and quiet demeanor. To my complete surprise and relief, those thoughts and fears were not coming from the Giver of life. God injected His life into me to the brim and has given me more peace and joy than I knew existed. Even in the most difficult of times, He comforts me. Each day brings new challenges and opportunities to love God, to grow and love and encourage others along the way. The best part is that I do not have to pretend that I am perfect. When I do mess up, I am a breath away from receiving forgiveness by confessing it to God and putting whatever it was behind me. What is the value of being a child of God with the Spirit living in us? Priceless! ✈

Unanswered

CHAPTER FIFTEEN
A BEAUTIFUL LIE

Chapter 15: A Beautiful Lie

When I first became a believer and was trying to make sense of my newfound life, I bumped into a friend who had heard that I had become one of those "born againers." He couldn't believe that I would give in to such nonsense and said, "I always thought that you were a lot smarter than that!" "Christianity is not garbage, nor is it a covey of freaks; it is the truth, pure and simple!" I said, thinking that my response would put an end to this conversation that was going nowhere. "Anybody from any religion could make that claim," he responded. I was dumbfounded. I did not have a response for his comment. I did not know how to defend my faith because I had not done my homework. I was upset; I should have had a response, but I didn't.

"But in your hearts set apart Christ as Lord. Always be prepared to give an answer to everyone who asks you to give the reason for the hope that you have. But do this with gentleness and respect, keeping a clear conscience, so that those who speak maliciously against your good behavior in Christ may be ashamed of their slander" (1 Peter 3:15-16).

I'm sure that I am not the only one who has been caught unprepared when confronted with questions about the veracity of Christianity. I thank God for that conversation, because it made me search even harder for the truth. I was determined that the next time it happened (and it did), I would be prepared to give a truthful answer with gentleness and respect.

For some reason, few Christians think that it is necessary to study the foundations of their faith. "Why should we?" some might ask. The answer is simple: once you become a Christ follower, it is no longer all about you. It is now about preparing yourself to become well grounded so that you can be a light and a responder to those who are seeking to know God. If we know the foundations of our faith, we will not only strengthen our own faith in God, but also be prepared to have conversations with those who are seeking answers that can help them better understand Christianity. People today are being bombarded with all kinds of opinions and theories that make little sense. Unless we know the truth about God, the Bible, Jesus, and His death and resurrection, we will not be prepared to speak truth into these conversations, and many will fall away from their faith. Sadly enough, the majority of Christians do not know enough about their faith to get into these conversations in the first place.

The result of all of this is that people are not being given answers to their questions, so they stop pursuing God. Today's young men and women (up to 80 percent) are walking away from their faith in God by the time they graduate from college because they were not taught the foundations of their faith. These students who cannot defend their faith fall victim to intimidation from professors and atheist friends.

The very best defense of the Christian faith is to know the truth, really know it, and not just be familiar with it. Then we can engage in conversations that will not only answer others' questions, but will also afford us the opportunity to kindly challenge their own belief system. Our hope is that, by engaging with a person who is considering the Christian faith, we might give them much to think about and be able to continue with conversations, not debates, down the road. Our goal is for Christians to embrace questions with the hope that their answers would move the person asking closer to a faith in Christ.

The following four "Deadly Questions" have proven to be extremely effective to ask those who are attacking or challenging your faith. They are also useful in pointing out the error of thinking in someone else's point of view.[1] I strongly encourage you to memorize these and prepare to use them whenever you encounter adversity, be it at work, during lunch, at a meeting, or just hanging out with friends. You will find that, as you familiarize yourself with these questions, they will become a natural part of your conversations without having to work at it.

1. **What do you mean by that?**

Any time that you want to get into a discussion with someone, make sure that the terms are defined. Often the discussion will end here if there is a misunderstanding of words. You will fast weed out those who just want to argue and have no clue about the issue.

If someone says, "Only idiots would believe that God inspired the writing of the Bible," your response might be, "What do you mean by 'idiots' and what do you mean by 'inspired'?"

2. **How do you know that is true?**

Surprisingly, most people believe things for which they have absolutely no evidence. Try this question out on someone with strong opinions and be ready for a fascinating discussion.

In this particular case the question would be, "Do you know all the 'idiots' in the world? If not, then how can you make such a statement?" Then ask, "How do you know that the Bible is not inspired by God? What is your evidence?"

3. **Where do you get your information?**

When someone makes a radical claim, you should always ask detailed questions about how they know what they know. Before long, you will get to the end of their knowledge and be on even terms in the discussion.

"Have you read the Bible? What exactly are the verses that you are holding in question? Have you considered the prophecies in the Bible, all 2,000 of them? How many of those have come true? Is that mathematically possible or probable?" Chances are that you will not get beyond the first question. I would then encourage them to do their homework and offer them some good sources for truth, like this book!

4. What happens if you are wrong?

It is one thing to claim a belief, and yet another to stake your life on it. The most important question that can be asked in life is, "Where do you go when you die, and what happens if you are wrong?"

When dealing with the argument that God did not inspire the writing of the Bible, a good rebuttal to this might be, "If by chance you are wrong about Christians and about the Bible, then consider that the Bible tells the story of God's love for all people. He offers eternal life in heaven with Him to all who choose to believe in Him. For those who do not believe in Jesus and His sacrificial death on the cross to pay the price for all of our sins, God will give them the desire of their heart—they will live forever without God, resulting in total darkness and torment. In spite of your unbelief, God loves you and wants you to believe in Him. Are you content in being where you are or are you interested in at least entertaining the idea that there is a God who loves you?"

I was talking with a youth pastor and friend, and he mentioned that he disagreed with the idea of biblical creationism that we teach in the Anchorsaway curriculum. I asked him why he rejected the idea of God being the creator of the world. He said that he believed that God started creation, but then evolution kicked in. This is what is known as theistic evolution. Knowing that the biblical account of creation is true, I wanted to argue with him, but instead asked him what he meant by evolution. He said that he believed that it was a combination of random chance and God. I then asked him how he knew it was true. He said he had received this information from one of his college professors at a well-known Christian college in Chicago. I probed a little more and asked him if he believed everything that professors, even in Christian colleges, teach. He didn't answer, and then I continued by asking him, "I know what your professor believes, but what you are telling me is that your source for rejecting God's Word is one teacher's opinion. Don't you think you owe it to yourself, to the Lord, and to your students to look into this issue for yourself? I will give you some books to study if you would like, but please, would you study it for yourself?" That was the end of the conversation. To this day, he continues to pass on what was passed on to him—that God was only a part of the creation story, thus undermining the veracity of the Scriptures and setting his students up for much confusion, and for some, a walk away from their faith.

"Not many of you should presume to be teachers, my brothers, because you know that we who teach will be judged more strictly" (James 3:1).

A great exercise to use when confronted by an atheist (one who denies that there is a God) or an agnostic (one who will acknowledge the possibility of a God) is what I call, C.S. Lewis's "Dot-in-the-circle" diagram.[2]

You can use this when someone makes an outrageous statement such as, "There is no God." Take some time to have a conversation with them and hopefully answer some of their questions, and maybe ask some of your own. It should be a friendly atmosphere. You can either draw a circle out on a napkin while having coffee with a friend, or it can be talked out with no visual.

You might say, "The space inside the circle represents all experience and all knowledge from all times here on earth." Ask your friend to mark in the circle how much knowledge they have as compared to all knowledge, wisdom, and truth for all time. They will most likely put a very small dot in the circle. Then ask, "Outside of all the knowledge that you have, might there be something that you have yet to experience?" The friend will no doubt say that there is. Then follow up with, "I am not saying there is, but could their possibly be a God who created you and loves you beyond your wildest dreams?" The idea here is to have the atheist see that there are occurrences, perhaps even truths that exist beyond his or her own personal experience. This opens the door to plant a seed of doubt in their mind that might cause the person to question his or her godless faith and allow you to open a dialog with them about the possibility of a personal God, who loves them. If the time is right, extend an invitation to meet again and take a closer look to see if there might be such a God!

I use this often in many different situations. Someone may say that all creationists are ignorant of science. My response is, "Do you know all the creationists in the world?" Answer: "No." "Might there be, beyond your knowledge, someone who is a scientist who believes in Creation?"

Practice these questions on your friends, and then on those who are attacking your ideas. Remember, the goal is not to win a debate, but rather ask questions that will cause the listener to think! Then, have your friends turn the tables on you, and ask you the deadly questions to some of your truth claims. This is a great exercise to build up your confidence, not only in confronting others, but in your own faith, as well! ✈

CHAPTER SIXTEEN
CHARADES

Chapter 16: Charades

Who is Satan? Is he real? Is he merely a figment of someone's fantasy that we see at the movies, or should we take notice of him? Statistics tell us that 65 percent of Christians believe that the Devil or Satan is not a living being, but merely a symbol of evil.[1] As we study the Scriptures, we will find that, contrary to what most Christians believe, he is very real and extremely active in the world today.

"We know that we are from God, and the whole world lies in the power of the evil one" (1 John 5:19).

Those of us who are walking with Christ with a strong foundation of faith know that Satan has no power over us. This, however, does not mean that he won't try to derail our trust in God. The good news is that God has equipped us to win the battle when Satan tries to attack us. He is a threat to all of us because he uses subtlety and deception to carry out his plans. Satan's consuming desire is to pull us away from God, and he will go to any length to do so.

From where did Satan come? Ezekiel 28:11-19 and Isaiah 14:12-20 tell us of Satan's rise and fall from heaven. In the book of Ezekiel, he writes to the king of Tyre who was blatantly practicing paganism. He was steeped in the occult, and as a result, God was going to bring down the beautiful city of Tyre and its king, who was filled with wickedness and pride (Ezekiel 28:2-6). As God predicts the fall of the city and its king, He also speaks to the prophet, Ezekiel, about how Lucifer, God's highest angel and model of perfection, had fallen. Lucifer and the king of Tyre were very similar in their beauty, wisdom and pride. Both abandoned God, both were violent, and both wanted to be worshiped as a "god." Because of the similarities of character between the two, it is not surprising that God instructed Ezekiel to write about the fate of Lucifer. Ezekiel shares the details of his fate: of the garden, the holy mount of God, and of God throwing him (Lucifer) to the earth. In the end, God will expose Satan for who he is and will fulfill His prophecy to breathe fire on Satan, reducing him to ashes as he comes to a dreadful end. The Ezekiel and Isaiah passages are the only passages that give us much detail about Lucifer/Satan, as we know him today.

"Moreover, the word of the LORD came to me: 'Son of man, raise a lamentation over the king of Tyre, and say to him, thus says the Lord GOD: "You were the signet of perfection full of wisdom and perfect in beauty. You were in Eden, the garden of God; every precious stone was your covering, sardius, topaz, and diamond, beryl, onyx, and jasper, sapphire, emerald, and carbuncle; and crafted in gold were your settings and your engravings. On the day that you were created they were prepared. You were an anointed guardian cherub. I placed you; you were on the holy mountain of God; in the midst of the stones of fire you walked. You were blameless in your ways from the day you were created, till unrighteousness was found in you. In the abundance of your trade you were filled with violence in your midst, and you sinned; so I cast you as a profane thing from the mountain of God, and I destroyed you, O guardian cherub, from the midst of the stones of fire. Your heart was proud because of your beauty; you corrupted your wisdom for the sake of your splendor. I cast you to the ground; I exposed you before kings, to feast their eyes on you. By the multitude of your iniquities in the unrighteousness of your trade you profaned your sanctuaries; so I brought fire out from your midst; it consumed you, and I turned you to ashes on the earth in the sight of all who saw you. All who know you among the peoples are appalled at you; you have come to a dreadful end and shall be no more forever"'" (Ezekiel 28:11-19).

"How you are fallen from heaven, O Day Star, son of Dawn! How you are cut down to the ground, you who laid the nations low! You said in your heart, 'I will ascend to heaven; above the stars of God I will set my throne on high; I will sit on the mount of assembly in the far reaches of the north; I will ascend above the heights of the clouds; I will make myself like the Most High.' But you are brought down to Sheol, to the far reaches of the pit. Those who see you will stare at you and ponder over you: 'Is this the man who made the earth tremble, who shook kingdoms, who made the world like a desert and overthrew its cities, who did not let his prisoners go home?' All the kings of the nations lie in

glory, each in his own tomb; but you are cast out, away from your grave, like a loathed branch, clothed with the slain, those pierced by the sword, who go down to the stones of the pit, like a dead body trampled underfoot. You will not be joined with them in burial, because you have destroyed your land, you have slain your people. May the offspring of evildoers nevermore be named" (Isaiah 14:12-20).

Satan's future was sealed. He would be thrown from heaven where he would exist with the demons (fallen angels) that had also turned from God and worshiped Lucifer.

"Now war arose in heaven, Michael and his angels fighting against the dragon. And the dragon and his angels fought back, but he was defeated, and there was no longer any place for them in heaven. And the great dragon was thrown down, that ancient serpent, who is called the devil and Satan, the deceiver of the whole world—he was thrown down to the earth, and his angels were thrown down with him" (Revelation 12:7-9).

Our first introduction to Satan is in Genesis 3, where he tempted Eve and then Adam to disobey God. Thus the birth of sin whose effects we experience every day in disease, physical and emotional suffering, and death. The first lie that Satan spoke to Eve planted doubt in her mind, and introduced the thought that man too could become like God. We'll discuss this in detail in Chapter 17: The Killing Field.

"Now the serpent was more crafty than any other beast of the field that the LORD God had made. He said to the woman, 'Did God actually say, "You shall not eat of any tree in the garden"?' And the woman said to the serpent, 'We may eat of the fruit of the trees in the garden, but God said, "You shall not eat of the fruit of the tree that is in the midst of the garden, neither shall you touch it, lest you die."' But the serpent said to the woman, 'You will not surely die. For God knows that when you eat of it your eyes will be opened, and you will be like God, knowing good and evil'" (Genesis 3:1-5).

Satan's whole purpose is to stop us from worshiping and following God. From the looks of things, Satan and his demons are doing a great job. As we look at the world today, we see the continued fallout of people turning from God. Satan used his pride, greed, deceit and craftiness to successfully cause the fall from grace, which is still the root of the chaos that reigns throughout the world today. Every single cult promises that you can become a "god" and choose your own value and moral system. All of this goes against the very heart of God and undoubtedly grieves Him to see so many falling into Satan's trap. The death and resurrection of Jesus paid the price for all sin and gave us freedom from being under Satan's control. Christ reigns victorious over Satan and his demons both now and forever!

"I will not execute my burning anger; I will not again destroy Ephraim; for I am God and not a man, the Holy One in your midst, and I will not come in wrath" (Hosea 11:9).

"But now that you have been set free from sin and have become slaves of God, the fruit you get leads to sanctification and its end, eternal life. For the wages of sin is death, but the free gift of God is eternal life in Christ Jesus our Lord" (Romans 6:22-23).

"Little children, you are from God and have overcome them, for he who is in you is greater than he who is in the world" (1 John 4:4).

Names matter. We ponder the names for our children, which is a carryover from ancient biblical times. God gave names to others that reflect their character or something special about them.

"The man called his wife's name Eve, because she was the mother of all living" (Genesis 3:20).

"'She will bear a son, and you shall call his name Jesus, for he will save his people from their sins.' All this took place to fulfill what the Lord had spoken by the prophet: 'Behold, the virgin shall conceive and bear a son, and they shall call his name Immanuel' (which means, 'God with us')" (Matthew 1:21-23).

New Testament books, whose authors wrote under the inspiration of the Holy Spirit, are full of references to the names of Satan. His name means "adversary." The following declare the nature and heart of Satan:[2]

- **Tempter**. "And Jesus, full of the Holy Spirit, returned from the Jordan and was led by the Spirit in the wilderness for forty days, being tempted by the devil. And he ate nothing during those days. And when they were ended, he was hungry. The devil said to him, 'If you are the Son of God, command this stone to become bread.' And Jesus answered him, 'It is written, 'Man shall not live by bread alone...'" (Luke 4:1-4).

- **Angel of light.** "And no wonder, for even Satan disguises himself as an angel of light" (2 Corinthians 11:14).
- **Counterfeit Christian**. "Then he left the crowds and went into the house. And his disciples came to him, saying, 'Explain to us the parable of the weeds of the field.' He answered, 'The one who sows the good seed is the Son of Man. The field is the world, and the good seed is the sons of the kingdom. The weeds are the sons of the evil one, and the enemy who sowed them is the devil. The harvest is the end of the age, and the reapers are angels. Just as the weeds are gathered and burned with fire, so will it be at the end of the age. The Son of Man will send his angels, and they will gather out of his kingdom all causes of sin and all law-breakers, and throw them into the fiery furnace. In that place there will be weeping and gnashing of teeth. Then the righteous will shine like the sun in the kingdom of their Father. He who has ears, let him hear'" (Matthew 13:36-43).
- **Counterfeit Gospel.** "I am astonished that you are so quickly deserting him who called you in the grace of Christ and are turning to a different gospel—not that there is another one, but there are some who trouble you and want to distort the gospel of Christ" (Galatians 1:6-7).
- **Counterfeit Righteousness** (by works and the law). "What shall we say, then? That Gentiles who did not pursue righteousness have attained it, that is, a righteousness that is by faith; but that Israel who pursued a law that would lead to righteousness did not succeed in reaching that law. Why? Because they did not pursue it by faith, but as if it were based on works. They have stumbled over the stumbling stone..." (Romans 9:30-32).

- **Counterfeit Ministers.** "For such men are false apostles, deceitful workmen, disguising themselves as apostles of Christ. And no wonder, for even Satan disguises himself as an angel of light. So it is no surprise if his servants, also, disguise themselves as servants of righteousness. Their end will correspond to their deeds" (2 Corinthians 11:13-15).
- **Counterfeit christs.** "Let no one deceive you in any way. For that day will not come, unless the rebellion comes first, and the man of lawlessness is revealed, the son of destruction, who opposes and exalts himself against every so-called god or object of worship, so that he takes his seat in the temple of God, proclaiming himself to be God" (2 Thessalonians 2:3-4).
- **Deceptive.** "Beware of false prophets, who come to you in sheep's clothing but inwardly are ravenous wolves" (Matthew 7:15).
- **The enemy.** "He said to them, 'An enemy has done this.' So the servants said to him, 'Then do you want us to go and gather them?' But he said, 'No, lest in gathering the weeds you root up the wheat along with them'" (Matthew 13:28-29).
- **Destroyer.** "The thief comes only to steal and kill and destroy. I came that they may have life and have it abundantly." (John 10:10); "They have as king over them the angel of the bottomless pit. His name in Hebrew is Abaddon, and in Greek he is called Apollyon" (Revelation 9:11).
- **Adversary, a roaring lion.** "Be sober-minded; be watchful. Your adversary the devil prowls around like a roaring lion, seeking someone to devour" (1 Peter 5:8).
- **Accuser.** "And I heard a loud voice in heaven, saying, 'Now the salvation and the power and the kingdom of our God and the authority of his Christ have come, for the accuser of our brothers has been thrown down, who accuses them day and night before our God'" (Revelation 12:10).

- **Liar and murderer.** "You are of your father the devil, and your will is to do your father's desires. He was a murderer from the beginning, and does not stand in the truth, because there is no truth in him. When he lies, he speaks out of his own character, for he is a liar and the father of lies" (John 8:44).
- **Prince of demons.** "But when the Pharisees heard it, they said, 'It is only by Beelzebul, the prince of demons, that this man casts out demons'" (Matthew 12:24).
- **Ruler of this world.** "Now is the judgment of this world; now will the ruler of this world be cast out" (John 12:31); "I will no longer talk much with you, for the ruler of this world is coming. He has no claim on me..." (John 14:30); "...concerning judgment, because the ruler of this world is judged" (John 16:11).
- **Prince of the power of the air.** "...in which you once walked, following the course of this world, following the prince of the power of the air, the spirit that is now at work in the sons of disobedience..." (Ephesians 2:2).
- **"god" of this age.** "In their case the god of this world has blinded the minds of the unbelievers, to keep them from seeing the light of the gospel of the glory of Christ, who is the image of God" (2 Corinthians 4:4).
- **Lawless one.** "And then the lawless one will be revealed, whom the Lord Jesus will kill with the breath of his mouth and bring to nothing by the appearance of his coming" (2 Thessalonians 2:8).
- **Devil.** "...for forty days, being tempted by the devil. And he ate nothing during those days. And when they were ended, he was hungry." (Luke 4:2); "And the great dragon was thrown down, that ancient serpent, who is called the devil and Satan, the deceiver of the whole world—he was thrown down to the earth, and his angels were thrown down with him" (Revelation 12:9).
- **Blinder of minds.** "In their case the god of this world has blinded the minds of the unbelievers, to keep

them from seeing the light of the gospel of the glory of Christ, who is the image of God" (2 Corinthians 4:4).

- **Unclean spirit**. "When the unclean spirit has gone out of a person, it passes through waterless places seeking rest, but finds none" (Matthew 12:43).
- **Serpent**. "And the great dragon was thrown down, that ancient serpent, who is called the devil and Satan, the deceiver of the whole world—he was thrown down to the earth, and his angels were thrown down with him" (Revelation 12:9).
- **Beezlebub**. "But some of them said, "He casts out demons by Beelzebul, the prince of demons..." (Luke 11:15).
- **The evil one.** "And lead us not into temptation, but deliver us from evil" (Matthew 6:13); "We know that we are from God, and the whole world lies in the power of the evil one" (1 John 5:19).

The names Satan, Devil, demons and evil spirits are mentioned 165 times in the New Testament. Why does Jesus go to such extremes to make sure that we know who Satan is and how he works? It is because God loves us and does not want us to fall for his ploys. Satan is not to be taken lightly. He is for real and is bent on destroying all of us. He hates you and me, Jesus, the Holy Spirit and the Father. He has absolutely no boundaries and will attack anyone at any time. He is not a respecter of people, time, age, pain or suffering. When we are not walking close to God, we are extremely vulnerable to his attack. That is why it is acutely important that we are in the Scriptures and in communion with God, so that we will not be deceived by Satan's voice, but rather will know and listen only to the voice of God.

"Now these Jews were more noble than those in Thessalonica; they received the word with all eagerness, examining the Scriptures daily to see if these things were so. Many of them therefore believed, with not a few Greek women of high standing as well as men" (Acts 17:11-12).

The Christ follower cannot be possessed by Satan because the Holy Spirit dwells in us, but we certainly can be oppressed, meaning Satan can attack but cannot take up residency in us. Satan can, and often does, possess the unbeliever who has rejected Christ and who opens him or herself to the things of Satan, like participating in séances, Ouija boards, occult paraphernalia, Satanic video games, satanic sites on the internet, and a steady diet of satanic movies and books. He is at the epicenter of the New Age movement, which so many of today's churches have bought into and promote. Satan is a formidable adversary. He is an enemy who is as subtle as a serpent and as strong as a lion, who is able to appear as an angel of light. Our God, however, is not surprised or intimidated by him, but has great power over him. Satan and his demons had a beginning and they will suffer a ghastly end.

"And the beast was captured, and with it the false prophet who in its presence had done the signs by which he deceived those who had received the mark of the beast and those who worshiped its image. These two were thrown alive into the lake of fire that burns with sulfur" (Revelation 19:20).

Many of us would say that we do not play in Satan's arena, but there are times when we all reflect the darkness of Satan rather than the light of Christ. Interestingly enough, several of the characteristics of Satan are what Scripture defines as our sin nature. Many of these things come naturally to us, and when we choose to speak and behave in ways we know we shouldn't, we tend to dismiss them as being unimportant and inconsequential. Those attitudes and actions that do not come from God might include such things as lying, anger, stealing, pride, slander, gossiping, getting even, disrespecting someone, condescension and worry. They seem little to us, but to the person looking for God who sees us during times like this, it often becomes a huge stumbling block. Again, the closer we walk with God, the more we will be aware of our choices and the power that lives in us to not sin in these ways. Satan is never, ever an excuse for us to sin. The Devil can't make you do it. God tells us to have nothing at all to do with Satan, but be a light to those in darkness.

"Take no part in the unfruitful works of darkness, but instead expose them. For it is shameful even to speak of the things

that they do in secret. But when anything is exposed by the light, it becomes visible, for anything that becomes visible is light. Therefore it says, 'Awake, O sleeper, and arise from the dead, and Christ will shine on you'" (Ephesians 5:11-14).

Caution must be used when choosing to peel back the layers behind Satan. We must be careful not to see Satan behind everything, but on the other hand, it is equally dangerous to believe he does not exist—there must be a balance. It is essential to undergo a healthy study of him so that the foundation of our faith is strong. Without understanding who he is and how to fight him, we would be doing a grave disservice to ourselves and to those who want to learn.

Unanswered

CHAPTER SEVENTEEN
THE KILLING FIELD

Chapter 17: The Killing Field

It is not our desire to give Satan any credit whatsoever, but to say that Satan does not exist is as silly as saying that he will not attack Christians. His primary desire is to take the eyes and hearts of Christ followers off of Christ. From the beginning of time, Satan has proven that he is a very cunning liar, and will stop at nothing to keep us from having a vibrant relationship with God. He wages a spiritual war on us that cannot be won with normal weapons of warfare. He also attacks in diverse ways that make him much harder to recognize and defeat.

"Put on the whole armor of God, that you may be able to stand against the schemes of the devil. For we do not wrestle against flesh and blood, but against the rulers, against the authorities, against the cosmic powers over this present darkness, against the spiritual forces of evil in the heavenly places" (Ephesians 6:11-12).

"Be sober-minded; be watchful. Your adversary the devil prowls around like a roaring lion, seeking someone to devour" (1 Peter 5:8).

Before we get too far into this study, let us all agree on one thing: busyness is not from God, but rather one of Satan's most effective tools in most of our lives. Making sure we are busy appeals to our flesh and our pride. In our culture, more is better on so many levels: the larger house, classier car, sharper clothes, bigger income, and trimmer bodies can all define us. We make time to do the things we think are important while putting off the things we think can wait, like spending time with God in prayer and reading the Scriptures. We think it really doesn't matter all that much, but as we work through this lesson, we will find that this way of thinking just might be the reason so many of us struggle to live life to the full from God's perspective. Having an active prayer and Scripture reading life is critical. These disciplines help us learn the voice of the Lord, so we will not be easily confused when we hear the thoughts of Satan trying to counter the truth of God. By learning some of the ways that Satan attacks us, we will better recognize his voice and reject the thoughts he puts into our minds. He is effective because he speaks our language, and, if we listen to it as truth, it can and often does cause havoc in our lives.

One of Satan's most effective tools is discouragement. God plants an idea in our minds and Satan is right behind Him telling us things like, "It will never work. You aren't smart enough to do it. Remember all the other screw-ups? He is not going to use you. You are destined for failure and God knows it!" Perhaps this will sound familiar. "You are such a loser. God only uses people like so-and-so. You do not, nor will you ever, make the grade. Just give up." Or how about this one: "Terrible job. You really messed that one up. You made a complete fool of yourself." No doubt we have had some of these thoughts. How do we know these words are not true, that they are not from God, but from Satan? Satan will always attack our character. God will never attack our character, but will convict us of our sin. Satan's attacks are meant to destroy and discourage while God's words of conviction are intended to restore and give life.

"The thief comes only to steal and kill and destroy. I came that they may have life and have it abundantly. I am the good shepherd… My sheep hear my voice, and I know them, and they follow me. I give them eternal life, and they will never perish, and no one will snatch them out of my hand" (John 10:10-11a, 27-28).

Another ploy of Satan's is that he whispers to us that we are not forgiven. All of us have done and said things that were hurtful and clearly not of God. We have had moments of being a bad witness to others and to God. We have caused people to say, "What a hypocrite!" because we were. We have gossiped, lied, cheated, coveted and have cared more about the impression we made on others than we did in honoring and bringing glory to our Lord. When God, or someone else, brings behavior like this to our attention, we must immediately go to God and agree with Him that we have sinned and ask Him to forgive us. God is pleased to forgive us when we come to Him. We can know for sure that when we ask, he will forgive. Period. As a matter of fact, God even chooses to forget what He has just forgiven.

"If we confess our sins, he is faithful and just to forgive us our sins and to cleanse us from all unrighteousness" (1 John 1:9).

"The LORD is merciful and gracious, slow to anger and abounding in steadfast love. He will not always chide, nor will he keep his anger forever. He does not deal with us according to our sins, nor repay us according to our iniquities. For as high as the heavens are above the earth so great is his steadfast love toward those who fear him as far as the east is from the west, so far does he remove our transgressions from us" (Psalm 103:8-12).

Satan, as usual, tries to trump the Word of God with a lie. Even when we go to those whom we have offended and ask for forgiveness, he often whispers to us once again that we are not forgiven and continues to bring the sin or situation to our minds for us to replay continually. As a result, our faith weakens, anxiety rises, and our joy diminishes. As we have learned about the character of God, He is true to His Word—when He says we are forgiven, we are forgiven. It is up to us to choose to believe it!

The same kind of deception reigns in the minds of many who have responded to God's call of trusting Him. Satan uses the same tactic that he did to cause Eve to doubt, by whispering to us that just because God said something, that doesn't mean it is true. For many new Christians, Satan convinces them that, although we think and tell others we are Christ followers, we are not. We begin to doubt. We tell God again that we believe in Him, and again the voice tells us that we are not His. The cure for this is to tell God that you are sorry that you doubted His Word that says, *"whoever believes in him may have eternal life" (John 3:16).* Set your mind, once and for all, whether you feel it or not, on the truth that you are adopted and sealed by God to be His child forever.

In the Old Testament book of Job, we read that Job hung around with some friends who were misrepresenting God by saying things to Job that were not true. Satan can and does use even our friends to discourage us and bring us down.

They can misrepresent God and tell us things that are simply not true. Many churches are guilty of the same thing. Yes, it is good to go to a Bible-believing church and become involved. You are, however, no less of a Christian by not going or not becoming involved. The same is true of so many church traditions, which may be good things to do that honor God, but do not determine whether or not you are a Christian. That is one of the beauties of our faith in Jesus; our relationship is solely dependent on His amazing grace!

"By this you know the Spirit of God: every spirit that confesses that Jesus Christ has come in the flesh is from God, and every spirit that does not confess Jesus is not from God. This is the spirit of the antichrist, which you heard was coming and now is in the world already" (1 John 4:2-3).

The good news for us is that Satan can try to confound and confuse our minds and do his best to get our eyes off our Lord, but he has no power to force us to do anything. Because God lives in us, we have at our disposal all the weapons we need to successfully fight off the temptations of the Devil. The Deceiver tries to make us believe that he can control us and is greater than God. We know Satan has no power over us—that issue was forever settled by Christ's death on the cross and followed by His resurrection! He lives! Our Savior lives!

"Little children, you are from God and have overcome them, for he who is in you is greater than he who is in the world. They are from the world; therefore they speak from the world, and the world listens to them. We are from God. Whoever knows God listens to us; whoever is not from God does not listen to us. By this we know the Spirit of truth and the spirit of error" (1 John 4:4-6). Not only does God equip us with His power to fight the good fight, but He also tells us how to stand up against Satan's attacks.

"Finally, be strong in the Lord and in the strength of his might. Put on the whole armor of God, that you may be able to stand against the schemes of the devil. For we do not wrestle against flesh and blood, but against the rulers, against the authorities, against the cosmic powers over this present darkness,

against the spiritual forces of evil in the heavenly places. There-
fore take up the whole armor of God, that you may be able to
withstand in the evil day, and having done all, to stand firm.
Stand therefore, having fastened on the belt of truth, and having
put on the breastplate of righteousness, and, as shoes for your feet,
having put on the readiness given by the gospel of peace. In all
circumstances take up the shield of faith, with which you can ex-
tinguish all the flaming darts of the evil one; and take the helmet
of salvation, and the sword of the Spirit, which is the word of
God, praying at all times in the Spirit, with all prayer and sup-
plication. To that end keep alert with all perseverance, making
supplication for all the saints" (Ephesians 6:10-18).

Notice that our defense is a strong offense. This battle is one in which we need the "whole armor of God" in order to fight effectively and stand firm. There is nothing beyond God Himself that we need to defend ourselves. Although the writer of Ephesians, the Apostle Paul, was using the equipment of a fully armed Roman soldier, he was using these metaphors for the spiritual resources that have already been given to all believers. Retreating is not an option here. We are told to face the Enemy head on the same way we are encouraged to face our fears. God has already fully equipped us from head to foot with the truth, righteousness, the gospel, faith, salvation and the Word of God. The shield of faith will stave off attacks. The sword of the Spirit is the Word of God.

Note the importance of the Word of God. It is the only offensive weapon mentioned in this list. When we use Scripture to confront Satan's attacks, we speak it through the power of the Holy Spirit. Satan cannot stay and fight in the face of God's Word. Notice also when Satan was trying to tempt Jesus, with every statement Satan made, Jesus replied with the truth from the Scriptures. Yes, the Word of God is powerful, as powerful as a double-edged sword.

There is no doubt that God wants us to live a full life as we experience the fruit of the Spirit, which is love, joy, peace, patience, kindness, goodness, faithfulness, gentleness and self-control. That does not have to be taken from us by Satan's attacks. God has fully equipped us to win the battle against darkness with His Word. Without knowing the Word, we will struggle with our spiritual life as well as with our life in general. This should serve as a wake-up call to all of us to make our faith in God our top priority—time in the Word is not an option, but a must! ✈

Unanswered

CHAPTER EIGHTEEN

IDENTITY THEFT

Chapter 18: Identity Theft

The final straw was when my husband needed some gas for the lawn mower. He went to the gas station and filled up a five-gallon can to the top, put it in the back of his car and drove home. When he got home and opened the back door, he realized that the gas had spilled, soaking the carpet. The whole car, including the garage, reeked with gas fumes. It was a similar situation with the fertilizer bags he brought home for the garden that tore open in transport and the occasional dead animal he trapped that left their marks as well. With his birthday approaching, I found the answer to these never-ending car issues. I would go to the auction and buy him a used pickup truck. I had never been to a car auction before, so I took a friend with me, who also knew nothing about trucks, and off we went. We looked through the lot , and I found the perfect truck! It was red and shiny with not too many dents. The seats looked good and it had a radio, so I bid on it and got it! There weren't too many others bidding on this one, so I felt that I got a great deal. Too good to be true! I signed the papers and got in it to drive it home. It started up, but I noticed that when I shifted it into gear, it ground a bit, and when I pushed on the brakes, they were a bit soft. "That must be what trucks are like," I thought. By the grace of God, it made it home. I put a huge bow on the hood, and the kids and I waited expectantly for the birthday boy to see it. We hid it in the garage and hoped that he would be as excited as we all were with the perfect gift!

We waited with great expectation for his reaction! Soon he arrived and we made him turn away as we opened the garage door to unveil the red beauty! He was surprised all right. He and the kids piled into to it to take it for a test drive. The happy faces waved as he drove out of the driveway, only to return a very short time later. Ed said that he had to cut the test drive short because he wasn't convinced it was safe enough to drive on the streets. The next day, he took it to a mechanic who said, among other things, that the transmission was bad, the brake pads needed replacing and that it was not worth the gas that was in the tank. It was, as Ed described it, "the perfect storm"! We ended up returning the truck and getting one that had a good engine with tires and brakes that worked. It was not, however, as pretty as the other one, but it no doubt was the better choice.

It was not the first nor the last time that I was deceived by the way something looked on the outside, only to realize that, on the inside, it was rotten to the core. Scripture tells us that Satan often presents himself as beautiful, righteous and loving, but on the inside he is always a cunning liar whose mission is to seek and destroy.

"For such men are false apostles, deceitful workmen, disguising themselves as apostles of Christ. And no wonder, for even Satan disguises himself as an angel of light. So it is not strange if his servants also disguise themselves as servants of righteousness. Their end will correspond to their deeds" (2 Corinthians 11:13-15).

Not only does Satan disguise himself as a servant, a friend, a stranger, and even an angel, but also as a leader, a pastor or minister, a Bible teacher, or anyone else that we would trust to speak truth to us. That is why it is critical that we all have a firm foundation of truth so we will not be taken captive by Satan's lies and hollow promises. This faith foundation also allows us to be a voice of reason for those who have been lured into his trap. As we have said before, any cult or false religion will hold fast to the precept that Jesus is **not** God but that you can become one!

Because Satan is not a creative being but rather an imitator, his model for a cult is relatively consistent and fairly easy to spot if you know for what you are looking. Cults are a secretive way that Satan works through his unsuspecting victims. The definition of a "cult," from a Christian perspective, is a group of people centered on the false teachings of a leader who claims that he or she is uniquely called of God. A cult requires at least two people: a leader and a follower. In the United States, there are about 5,000 different types of cults. Some cults include only a few members, and you likely have never heard of them. Others, like the Mormons (called *The*

Church of Jesus Christ of Latter Day Saints), are so large that they have become a household name.

Scripture tells us that Satan is constantly at work "*looking for someone to devour*" (1 Peter 5:8). Ultimately, he is the originator of any philosophy, religion, or belief system that runs counter to God's Truth, often twisting reality so that it has a certain attraction to those who are unaware of his schemes. He will always mix his lies with some truth, even quoting Scripture, if necessary. Thousands of churched individuals are unknowingly drawn into cults. Satan is not a respecter of age, race, religion, social status or wealth. He will go after anyone and everyone. The most vulnerable are those who do **not** have their minds set on Christ, the Son of God, who do not have the Holy Spirit, or who are ignorant of the truth found in the Bible.

It is important to know some of the common characteristics of a cult.[1] The following is a brief list of things you might want to consider before you join a group that professes to be Christian. Not all groups possess all of these characteristics, but any one of them should be a warning to you to stay away.

- They will often reveal new truths that supersede or contradict the Bible.
- They have new interpretations of Scripture that are used to justify certain cultic beliefs.
- They use a non-biblical source of authority, whose sacred writings or authority often supersede the Bible, and worship another "Jesus," whom they see as a prophet, but not as God.
- They will present a new definition or complete denial of the Trinity.
- They believe that salvation is not by grace, but by works.
- The cult will revolve around a central leader who often will claim to have new revelations from God.

Our Postmodern culture is built on different versions of truth, making us vulnerable to the infiltration of various cults and false religions. Sadly, these cults, including Mormonism, have seduced millions of people into embracing their brand of truth. As we become aware of the different cults that exist, our vigilance will keep us from being persuaded to believe a lie. Furthermore, we will then be able to bring others into the light of God's truth.

Let's take a look at Mormonism. Why? It is one of the fastest growing counterfeit Christian religions in America today. More than 12 million people are members and over 63,000 are full-time missionaries. They are out knocking on doors and are extremely active on college campuses, which they see as breeding grounds for future Mormon members.

Agusta was Mormon for 15 years. She speaks to several groups and churches around the country as one of the leading experts on cults and Mormonism. The following is her testimony of how she became a Mormon, what it entailed, and how she escaped from it. Today, she and her husband have a ministry to Mormons and to those in other cults, as they devote their lives to loving and teaching them the truth about the real Jesus.

Agusta Harting's Story: "I was born and raised in Reykjavik, Iceland. Although my parents were not active in our Lutheran church, they still made me go to catechism (religious instructions) to be confirmed into the church at age 14. I came away from confirmation nearly as ignorant of the Christian faith as I had been before, only now I considered myself to be a 'Christian!'

The years passed, and when I turned 19, I met my husband, Dan, an American Navy officer who was stationed in Iceland for a few years. We moved to the U.S. and began raising our family of five children. Dan, who was raised a nominal Presbyterian, did not know much more about the Bible than I did. We carefully avoided going to church, politely declining if anybody we knew invited us to come along with them.

After ten years of marriage we were not happy, to say the least. I was beginning to feel empty and unfulfilled, no matter what worldly success we were enjoying. I had a very glamorous TV and modeling career, and Dan was fast climbing up the corporate ladder in a prestigious firm, making fistfuls of money as we went along. We had everything the world has to offer, but still I felt something was horribly missing in our lives.

One day, two Mormon missionaries showed up at our door. I eagerly invited them in, and they proceeded to teach me all about their church. I agreed to have them give me 'The Six Discussions,' as they call them; I was genuinely interested. Little did I know that I would not really be learning much about the bizarre teachings of this cult, but that I would be systematically led down the proverbial 'primrose path' to deception, thinking this was all 'Christianity,' in its purest form. The program I was being presented was carefully designed to make me agree quickly to be baptized into the 'only true church,' as Mormons call their Church of Jesus Christ of Latter Day Saints, or 'The Mormon Church,' as it is nicknamed by them and others.

At this point you might be wondering, 'Why is Mormonism so bad? Don't they call themselves Christians?' Please remember that I bear no grudge against any particular member of the Mormon Church. Like most other cultists, Satan has blinded them to the Truth of the real Gospel of Jesus Christ, and he holds them bound in this deception, which is both tricky and subtle. It is because I care about Mormons that I would have you be better equipped in witnessing to them about the real Jesus Christ of the Bible, whom they think they already represent.

The Mormons taught me that their movement, to which they refer as 'The Restoration,' began in 1820, when a young man who was 14 years old allegedly went into the woods to pray about which of all the churches in his vicinity he should join. His name was Joseph Smith, Jr.

I was told that no sooner had young Smith begun to pray, than a power so evil that he thought it would destroy him, seized upon him and bound his tongue. And just when he thought he would surely die, a pillar of light, brighter than the noonday sun, appeared above him. In the light stood two white-haired men, whom we are to assume to be God, the Father and his Son, Jesus Christ. Mormons call this event 'The First Vision,' and hang all the existence for their church and its 'restored gospel' upon it! (Naturally, I had no idea that there are 9 versions to this story, each differing greatly from the others.)

The 'official' version of this story records that the father and the son told Joseph Smith to join NONE of the churches found on the Earth, for they were ALL false! He was told that all statements of faith (creeds) in all of Christianity were a lie, false and abominable in God's sight. Also, that all those who professed faith in them were 'liars.'

After the Mormons told me this awesome story, they quietly and deliberately said, 'Sister Harting, we bear you our testimony that these things we have told you are true. And, by the power of the Holy Ghost you can come to know that they are true, also.' This 'testimony' was borne to me over 80 times in the following five discussions.

Later, they told me that Joseph Smith claimed that an angel had appeared in his bedroom, and told him that he (Joseph) would be the instrument that God would use in restoring the gospel to the Earth. It had supposedly been lost when the original twelve apostles of Jesus Christ died. Because I was ignorant about the Bible, I did not know that the Gospel of Jesus Christ was never lost, but is clearly laid out in 1 Corinthians 15:1-5, *'Now I would remind you, brothers, of the gospel I preached to you, which you received, in which you stand, and by which you are being saved, if you hold fast to the word I preached to you—unless you believed in vain. For I delivered to you as of first importance what I also received: that Christ died for our sins in accordance with the Scriptures, that he was buried, that he was raised on the third day in accordance with the Scriptures, and that he appeared to Cephas, then to the twelve.'*

The 'angel' told Joseph Smith that his name was Moroni, and that he and his people before him, had lived on the American continent from 600 BC to 431 AD. Moroni, the son of Mormon, was supposedly a great warrior in his Earth life, but he had now become an angel. The story goes that this angel of light led Joseph Smith to a place in the hill above the Smith's farm, and told him to dig there for some gold plates with curious engravings upon them, which Mormons claim was 'Reformed Egyptian' (a language which has never been known or heard of in all of history!).

Having been exposed to Spiritism in Iceland, I was ignorant of the fact that God strictly forbids any contact between the living and the dead. This is called 'necromancy,' and He declares that it is detestable in His sight! (See Deuteronomy 18:12.) I also failed to understand that men do not become angels when they die! Angels are an entirely different species than humans and serve a completely different purpose in God's plan of salvation. If Joseph Smith indeed saw anything, it was a deceiving spirit, or a demon. (2 Corinthians 11:14; 1 Timothy 4:1).

Now the young Elders gave me a copy of their famous book, 'The Book of Mormon,' and told me that it was the final fruit of Joseph's digging. By miraculous means, and with special 'stones set in bows' found with the plates, he was allegedly able to translate the golden plates into English, and published in 1830 what is now known as 'The Book of Mormon.' He also established the Mormon Church that same year.

I asked if I could see the golden plates, but the Elders answered that the angel had taken them to heaven, and that more plates would come forth some day. This sounded more than fishy to me! But Satan is clever and cultic powers are very seductive. Those sweet Elders implored me to pray about the truthfulness of the Book of Mormon. They simultaneously told me that the Bible had been translated so many times that it could have lost most of its meaning; it was definitely not a reliable book, according to them. On the contrary, Joseph Smith said in 1830 that The Book of Mormon was 'the most correct book on Earth and a man can get closer to God by living by its precepts than by any other book.' (I was not told that the B.O.M. had been changed in over 3,900 places without footnotes![2])

'Sister Harting, all you have to do is pray about it, and then listen to your heart! If you feel a burning in your bosom, you will have prayed honestly and can know the book is true!' Foolishly, and contrary to biblical warnings, I put this deceptive formula to the test and thought perhaps that I had 'felt something' in my bosom! The Bible says in Proverbs 28:26 (NKJV), 'He who trusts in his own heart is a fool, but whoever walks wisely will be delivered.'

Once I had convinced myself that the Book of Mormon was true, everything else fell into place like dominos. I was baptized by immersion by Mormon priests. I was told that only they had the authority to baptize anyone on earth. Peter, James and John, the Apostles of old, also supposedly came in person and ordained them to the Melchizedek Priesthood (even though the Bible declares in Hebrews 7 that Jesus ALONE holds this priesthood!) When I asked about the date of this great event, the missionaries hemmed and hawed and said that Joseph Smith had forgotten to write down the date!

I now thought that I had finally become a Christian. My husband soon followed suit, as did my son, who was 8 years old, the only one of our children at the time to qualify for Mormon baptism by being 'at the age of accountability.'

Time passed quickly, and eventually, we became isolated from all former friends and relatives by being kept so busy in the church; we had no time for anything else. Soon, we began to prepare to go to the Mormon Secret Temple to be 'sealed for time and all eternity.' Mormons consider this vital for gaining eternal life. Space prohibits me from describing the temple ritual in much detail, but nonetheless, it shocked me to no end.[3]

I will say that during this ungodly ceremony, we received 'secret names' and had to don ghoulish, Druid-like clothing, all in white, except for a bright green fig leaf apron, which we had to wear throughout the ritual. Worthy Mormons are even buried in this ghastly costume. We were shown a film depicting a typical Christian minister who was in the employ of Satan, and the main doctrines of the Christian faith were mocked. However, since 1990, Mormons have deleted some of the objectionable things from the ceremony, in order to make it more acceptable. Those 'oaths, signs and penalties' that we were made to perform had this intent: to give all our time, talents, and earthly goods over to the Mormon Church, as well as 'our lives, if necessary!' We were made to swear an oath never to reveal this 'sacred ritual.'

My family and I remained in the darkness of Mormonism until 1981. Then, God, by His infinite grace, allowed me to hear the REAL Gospel of Jesus Christ on the radio in Indianapolis, and I knew it was true! NOT because of my 'feelings,' or a 'burning in the bosom,' but because I carefully compared it with the Bible, God's ONLY authority on Earth! A short time later my husband, and every one of our children, left Mormonism. Most of our children are 'born again' Christians today.

In 1981, God called me and my husband to serve Him in the capacity of missionaries to Mormons and other cultists as well as equipping Christians in how to reach Mormons for Christ. Eventually, Families Against Cults was formed and we are currently working hard to bring other lost souls into the precious Kingdom of God, while we await the return of our precious Lord, Jesus Christ. He has graciously allowed us to see hundreds of cultists brought 'out of darkness into his wonderful light!' (1 Peter 2:9)."

I think that one of the most important things that all Christians need to know is that when someone is in a counterfeit Christian religion, the meaning of their words and phrases when compared to those of the Christian faith and the Bible appears very similar, but they are very different in meaning and application! So many people get swept into cults because they are tricked into thinking that it is just another very friendly Christian church that loves families and doesn't smoke or drink.

Check out the following, and please use this when talking with someone about Mormonism. These definitions are from their own writings:

1. **"God is my Father in Heaven."**

   Mormon meaning: God is a 6-foot-tall, physical "exalted man." His name is "Elohim." Once only a mere human, he had to learn to become god. He has a father, and there are many gods above him. He is only the "god of this universe."[4]

Christian meaning: Even though He is a personal Being, God, the Father has never been human. He is the Creator, and we are the created. God has created the entire universe. He is the head of the Trinity and all things are subject to Him; there is nothing, and no one, who is above Him (Isaiah 45:5-6; 1 Corinthians 15:27-28).

2. **"Jesus Christ is God's Son."**

Mormon meaning: Jesus Christ was a spirit baby born to Heavenly Father and one of his goddess wives, "Heavenly Mother." They named him "Jehovah." God is married to many women, and he cannot create anything from nothing. He had to have sex with his wife in order to produce Jesus pre-mortally, as well as all of humanity by the same method. Lucifer, the Devil, is also one of Jesus' "spiritual brothers."[5]

Christian meaning: Jesus, as God's Son, shares all of the qualities of God, Himself. He lacks nothing. As such, He never came into being because He has always been. In addition, Jesus has power over the Devil. The Devil has never been a spiritual equal of Jesus, as he is a fallen angel, and all angels are subject to Christ (Matthew 28:18; Luke 10:18-19; John 8:58; Colossians 1:15-18; Revelation 12:7-9).

3. **"The Holy Ghost is the third member of the Godhead."**

Mormon meaning: The Holy Ghost is a different god than Heavenly Father (Elohim). He has no physical body, and we do not know his name. He must not be confused with "The Holy Spirit," which is only like an impersonal electrical current.[6]

Christian meaning: In the history of Christianity, the title, "Holy Ghost," has frequently been interchangeable with the more common title, "Holy Spirit," when referring to the third member of the Trinity. They are not two separate entities, but instead, references to the same Being. The doctrine of the Trinity tells us that "God eternally exists as three persons, Father, Son, and Holy Spirit, and each person is fully God, and there is one God."[7] Therefore, the Holy Spirit is not a different God; He is God. He is a personal Being who has been sent to give us regeneration and help us live in obedience to God (Matthew 28:19; John 3:5-8; Ephesians 4:30 – Note: Only a personal Being can be "grieved.").

4. **"Jesus Christ is my Savior and Lord."**

Mormon meaning: Jesus (Jehovah) had to come to earth to complete his test of godhood. While here, he was married (possibly a polygamist)[8] and sweat blood in Gethsemane in order to "atone" for mankind and assure that we would all "gain resurrection bodies" someday. He is our "Elder Brother,"[9] and we must imitate him in order to earn and merit eternal life.

Christian meaning: Jesus did not earn His deity; He has always been God (Genesis 1:1; John 1:1-3). Yes, 1 John 2:6 tells us we must imitate Jesus by walking as He did, but our obedience to Christ is not a means to salvation. Salvation is a gift of God, which comes through our faith in Jesus' atoning sacrifice on the cross for our sins (Ephesians 2:8-9; 1 John 2:2).

5. **"Jesus was born of a virgin."**

Mormon meaning: God (Elohim) came down to Earth and had literal sexual intercourse with his virgin daughter, Mary. She thus conceived the earthly body for Jesus (Jehovah).[10]

Christian meaning: The Bible tells us that the Holy Spirit, not God, the Father, was the One who impregnated the virgin, Mary (Matthew 1:18-21; Luke 1:30-35). This was not a physical act of intercourse, but rather, a miraculous act of conception through the Holy Spirit.

6. "Jesus Christ is God."

Mormon meaning: Jesus Christ is a god, one of possibly billions of gods. Mormons are forbidden to worship or pray to him. They are not to have a "personal relationship" with him.[11]

Christian meaning: The Trinity doctrine tells us that there is only one God, not multiple gods. As a part of the Trinity, Jesus possesses the same divine characteristics of God the Father (John 8:58, 10:30). We are called to bow before Christ in worship and demonstrate our love for Him through our obedience to His commands (Philippians 2:9-11). Our personal relationship with Jesus is cultivated as we follow Him, in much the same way as He had a personal relationship with the 12 disciples during His three years of ministry on earth (John 10:27).

7. "Salvation is by God's grace through faith and works."

Mormon meaning: God only gives us the "grace" to be resurrected in a body of flesh and bone through Christ's sweating blood and death on the cross. Eternal life, however, must be EARNED and merited through personal worthiness.[12] This is called Eternal Progression to godhood. This is every Mormon's goal. The slogan in Mormonism is: "As man is, God once was; as God is, man may become!" [13]

Christian meaning: Scripture tells us that we have been saved through faith in God's gift of grace (Ephesians 2:8-9). We are not saved through our own merits. God has called us to come under His authority. When we seek to elevate ourselves above God, we sin against Him. (See the stories of Eve in Genesis 3:1-6 and the Tower of Babel in Genesis 11:1-9.)

8. "I believe in heaven and hell."

Mormon meaning: There are three "heavens." They are called the Celestial, Terrestrial and Telestial Kingdoms.[14] Most Christians and unworthy Mormons only qualify for the second, or the Terrestrial.[15] Worthy Mormons, who have become gods and goddesses, inherit the Celestial Kingdom. They will beget spirit children and populate their own earths and planets, just like Heavenly Parents did. The Telestial Kingdom is for the wicked, but still "glorious," according to Joseph Smith.

"Hell" is only a temporary prison for all non-Mormons until the resurrection. Great missionary work is being performed there right now.[16]

"Outer Darkness" is where the Devil and the demons go, as well as apostates who have left Mormonism and have become "Sons of Perdition." They remain there forever.

Christian meaning: The Bible speaks of only two eternal destinations for humanity—heaven or hell. They are both literal places, and Scripture does not suggest that there is more than one heaven. Hell is the place of eternal punishment for the wicked, while the righteous will enjoy eternal life in heaven (Matthew 25:46).

9. **"I believe the Bible is true, as far as it is translated correctly."**

Mormon meaning: The Bible was not translated correctly and there are many "plain and precious truths" missing in it, including whole books. According to Mormon Prophet Ezra T. Benson, it is not "big enough, nor good enough, to lead this [the Mormon] Church."

Christian meaning: The Bible is not only true, it is also without error. The three common tests for works of antiquity (bibliographic, internal, and external) confirm the authenticity of the Bible. More importantly, Scripture itself proclaims that every word has come from God, Himself (2 Timothy 3:16-17; 2 Peter 1:20-21). Therefore, it is pure, perfect, and true (Psalm 12:6, 119:96; Proverbs 30:5). There is nothing that needs to be added or taken away from God's Word; it is all we need for salvation (Deuteronomy 4:2, 12:32; Proverbs 30:5-6; Revelation 22:18-19).

10. "I believe in all the gifts of the Holy Ghost."

Mormon meaning: All spiritual gifts must be given from Joseph Smith, Jr. through the General Authorities of the Mormon Church, channeled down to the recipient by the laying on of hands by Mormon priests.[17]

Christian meaning: Scripture tells us that all gifts come from God and are bestowed upon us by the Holy Spirit, Himself (James 1:17; 1 Corinthians 12:1-11).[18]

I pray that you will clearly see the difference between Mormon teachings and the doctrine of the Christian faith! Please remember, in spite of the same terminology, Mormons worship a false god; they proclaim another (false) Jesus, and they teach a false gospel! To see how seriously God considers this, notice Paul's strong words:

"I am astonished that you are so quickly deserting the one who called you by the grace of Christ and are turning to a different gospel—which is really no gospel at all. Evidently some people are throwing you into confusion and are trying to pervert the gospel of Christ. But even if we or an angel from heaven should preach a gospel other than the one we preached to you, let him be eternally condemned! As we have already said, so now I say again: If anybody is preaching to you a gospel other than what you accepted, let him be eternally condemned!" (Galatians 1:6-9).

How could any intelligent, well educated and gifted person, like Agusta, believe in such things that cannot be proven by Scripture or by solid historical data? She was unhappy and desperate for some kind of hope—the Mormons knocked at her door and the rest was history. Although initially they did not tell her the truth of the Mormon religion, she became attracted to it because of the messengers, those who came to see her. The true goal of a Mormon is to become a god, while the goal of the Christian is to become conformed more to the image of Jesus. A god or a servant? Thinking that there really is such a choice, which there isn't, many choose to become a god. Why? They want to be worshiped and to rule over others, which is the same desire as Satan. Sadly enough for these people, someday, some dreadful day, they will stand before the One True God and realize, when it is too late, that they have worshiped a false god and that they will be separated forever from the One True God (Matthew 25:46, Matthew 7, John 8, Luke 16).

At first glance, Mormonism, like so many other cults, seems appealing. They are pro family, appear to be good people, and do not smoke, nor do they condone taking drugs. It is not until we take a closer, more intimate look below the surface of this cult, that we see the misguided beliefs and practices that exist. When we do learn more about characteristics of these cults, and hear the stories of those who have come out of them, we may mistakenly believe, "That will never happen to me."

This lesson is so important because there are thousands of people like Agusta being led astray because there was no Christian "knocking at their door". We all know people who are not Christ followers. God has called us to be a light in the world, to walk with those who are caught up in a cult so that they too can celebrate the freedom that they will have in Jesus. You can tell them about Jesus, about God Himself, who hung on a cross for the forgiveness of their sins. You can tell them about grace that God extends to all who will believe in His Son. Such words will overwhelm them as they realize that all the things they were doing to make God love them are now covered by grace! All that God requires of us after we believe is that we love God and love others! That, my friends, is very good news!

By the way. If anyone offers you a ride in a beautiful red truck, don't get in until you check it out! ✈

CHAPTER NINETEEN
THE GAMBLE

Chapter 19: The Gamble

As a university student, I was asked to fill out a questionnaire asking, among other things, which religion I practiced. With little thought, I checked Christian because I was a good American and knew I wasn't Jewish or Hindu. The results of the survey were reported in an article in the school newspaper stating that the vast majority of students on campus identified themselves as Christians. Several years later during my graduate studies, when I began to realize that educational degrees were not as fulfilling as I thought they might be, I started to re-evaluate my life journey. In the process, I wondered if I had mistakenly rejected God from my life. Perhaps He was real and if so, maybe I should reconsider my doubts of His existence and character. I remembered the study of all the Christians on campus who claimed to be Christ followers. It should have been easy to find someone who could answer some questions I had about God.

I wanted to know how my life might be different by believing in God. If there was hope and purpose in life? I found no one who gave me any reasonable answers to my questions. I concluded that their definition of a Christian was similar to mine: anyone who was born in America, attends church on Christmas Eve or on Easter and is a generally nice person, even if they have no idea what is fact or fiction about God. My assumption was that God is who you want Him to be, and that the weak-minded, or those brainwashed by their parents, would fall under the heading of "Christian."

Several years later, having finally found the answers to my questions, my decision to become a Christ follower was fairly simple. Through the process of studying the Christian faith, I began to better understand the confusion in the hearts and minds of many who have made faith claims. Consider the following categories of people of faith:

Group one are those who are saved by faith through Christ and know it. They are those who believe that Jesus Christ is God and that He died for their sins and rose again.

They have assurance that they are God's child, that the Bible is true and that when they die they will go to heaven. They are a reflection of God's love and grace.

Group two includes those who are saved by faith through Christ and do not know it. These people believe that Jesus Christ is God and that He died for their sins and rose again. They think that there must be something more that they must do or be in order to become one of His children. They do not understand grace. Most are convinced that following rules is what being a Christian is all about, which leaves them continually trying to win God's favor before and after they become Christ followers. Others in this group have been so beaten down by those around them, they believe the lie that says they are unworthy of God's love and grace. They simply do not know what to do with God's gift.

Group three are those who are not saved by faith through Christ and know it. This group is made up of individuals who have heard the truth of Christ and have knowingly rejected it. Their reasons for not pursuing faith in Jesus are many, including being turned off by the hypocrisy of those who claim to be Christians, the gospel has not been made clear to them or such a faith was not permitted in their family or by their friends. Many fear that to become a Christian they will have to commit intellectual suicide. They want to be in control and therefore have no choice left but to reject the belief of Jesus as Lord and Savior.

Group four are those who are not saved by faith through Christ and do not know it. They think that they are Christians, but are not. Many of these people are so performance minded that they believe being a Christian only involves going to church and following the rules. Many were raised in Christian homes and did what was expected of them, but never developed an authentic faith in God or a relationship with Him. They know how to speak Christianese, but their hearts are set on their own agenda. The hypocrites hide out in this group. They might attend Bible studies and go to church because it is "the thing to do," but inwardly their hearts are set on worldly things. They live in a world of duplicity (hypocrisy): being "religious" by going to the right church and serving on committees, but these things have little impact on how they live out their lives at work or at home.

This fourth group claim or think that they are Christians, but in reality are not, because they are ignorant regarding the commitment and statutes required by authentic faith. I believe that these are the people that the Barna Group reported who claimed to be Christian, but only six percent of them are living out the Christian worldview.[1] They would be identified as the worldview called Neo-Christianity. Neo-Christians have given an intellectual nod to Jesus Christ, with no heart commitment and no life change.

"By their fruit you will recognize them. Do people pick grapes from thorn bushes, or figs from thistles? Likewise every good tree bears good fruit, but a bad tree bears bad fruit. A good tree cannot bear bad fruit, and a bad tree cannot bear good fruit. Every tree that does not bear good fruit is cut down and thrown into the fire. Thus, by their fruit you will recognize them" (Matthew 7:16-20).

If God is convicting you, through the Holy Spirit, that you are one of the people in the fourth group, know that God is a God of second chances. He is calling you to an authentic faith in Him. He is asking you to come clean with Him and confess the emptiness of your heart and ask Him to cleanse you of all unrighteousness. There is nothing that you have done or that you have failed to do that God will not forgive.

"If we confess our sins, he is faithful and just to forgive us our sins and to cleanse us from all unrighteousness. If we say we have not sinned, we make him a liar, and his word is not in us" (1 John 1:9-10).

Sadly enough, I believe that a great number of traditional churchgoers fall into this category. I am encouraging—no—I am pleading with you to go before God and ask Him to examine your heart and reveal to you where you are in relation to His saving grace. This is between you and God alone. No other person can do anything about this issue. It is up to you. Take courage, be honest and, if necessary, repentant before God, and begin to live the life that God has planned for you, one of great peace and joy!

"Search me, O God, and know my heart! Try me and know my thoughts! And see if there be any grievous way in me, and lead me in the way everlasting" (Psalm 139:23-24).

What does it mean to be a person with an authentic faith in Jesus? A person does not become a Christian by feeling pressured to come forward at a church altar call and repeating a prayer that they really didn't understand. God is not impressed by words spoken, but rather by the heart of someone seeking after Him.

"The Lord does not look at the things man looks at. Man looks at the outward appearance, but the Lord looks at the heart" (1 Samuel 16:7).

If our words are not reflective of God's heart, then they fall on deaf ears. Becoming a Christian, a follower of Christ, is a gift from God by way of the cross, to all who choose to believe that Jesus Christ is God and the only Savior of the world.

"For God so loved the world that he gave his one and only Son, that whoever believes in him shall not perish but have eternal life" (John 3:16).

The Greek word for believe, *pisteuo*, means "to be persuaded of."[2] Therefore, to believe in Jesus is "to place confidence in, to trust" in Him. It is more than a mere credence; it requires a commitment to live out our faith in all areas of our lives. It is not an act; it is living out our faith gladly because of our gratefulness to God for all He has done for us.

The concept of a genuine belief in Christ might be understood through what I call the Potawatomi Principle. When I was in third grade, our class studied about the Potawatomi Indians who lived in Michigan. I learned about wigwams, the lodges that they lived in, and the food they ate. I loved looking at pictures of guys with mohawks and girls with beaded shirts. There was documented historical evidence, as well as artifacts, that proved beyond a shadow of a doubt that the Potawatomi Indians existed, and, as a matter of fact, still do today. I genuinely believed the Potawatomi Indians existed, but knowing all that information did not, and still does not in the least bit, influence how I think, or how I choose to spend my time, money and energy. Christ alone does.

Jesus established the criteria for living our lives. His disciples were called to, *"Come, follow me..."* *(Matthew 4:19a).* This invitation is extended so that we may become more like Christ. An authentic faith reflects a belief in and a commitment to Christ that is built on love and obedience. Scripture recorded how Christ showed us how to love and to live each day. As Christ was salt and light to the world, we, too, are called to imitate Christ (Matthew 5:13-16). The way we live should reflect the presence of the Holy Spirit, and bear witness to the authenticity of our faith and our loyalty to Jesus Christ (Galatians 5:22-25; 1John 2:6). God's will for our lives is to walk with Him, through the power of the Holy Spirit. In essence, we are called by God to live out the Christian worldview by loving Him and others in the most amazing ways!

We must make a choice. Maybe it is time, right now, to consider where you are in your relationship with Christ the Lord. If Christ is who He says He is, then the question is, "What are you going to do with Him?" He died to pay the penalty for your sin and to have an authentic relationship with you. He loves you! Trusting Him with your life is the first step as you grow in your relationship with Him. The more you trust, the more you grow. As with any new relationship, it takes time to know someone intimately—so it is with God. It does not mean that you will necessarily love Him wholeheartedly immediately; that will come in time. All He is asking is that you believe that He died for all of your sins: past, present and future, and He rose again! When you believe, He takes up residence in your soul and promises that you will live forever with Him in Heaven! That is the Gospel, the good news!

Others have been playing the "Christian" game, with one foot in heaven and the other foot in the world. In many ways, their behavior is no different from that of non-Christians. They are not a reflection of God, but rather, a reflection of the world. Christ says that we are either for Him or against Him; we cannot have both. It is either God or the world; He leaves that choice up to each one of us.

God not only is calling those who have never had a relationship with Him, but He is also calling those of us who are

Christians, but for whatever reason are burned out and have walked away from God as Lord. He wants us to ask for forgiveness and invite Him once again to be the Lord of our life.

God does know our hearts. If you would like to say a prayer affirming to God what you believe, do so. If you are wondering what such a prayer looks like, you can pray one like this: "Dear God, I believe that Jesus Christ died for my sins and that He rose again. I know that by believing this, I am promised eternal life, and that I can come to You from now on as Your child. Thank You for forgiving me and loving me just as I am. Make me into the person that You created me to be. Continue to reveal Yourself to me and to teach me what it is I need to know. In Jesus' name I pray. Amen."

If you believe that Jesus is God to the point that you are going to rely upon and trust God with the big and little things of your life, then let me assure you that you are God's child. You probably won't feel anything, but please know that, because of your faith, you are His child forever! Tell someone that you made a commitment, and start to learn about your Lord by finding someone who can mentor you in your faith. If you have made a commitment to Christ, I promise you it is the best decision that you have or ever will make!

Today is the day of salvation! *"Here I am! I stand at the door and knock. If anyone hears my voice and opens the door, I will come in..." (Revelation 3:20).*

Unanswered

CHAPTER TWENTY

NOW WHAT?

Chapter 20: Now What?

Have you ever had a vase of fresh cut flowers that look terrific, but after a few days, some began to wilt? After a few more days, you had to put the survivors in some new water and they continued to thrive for several more days. What makes some thrive and others not? The same might be asked about Christians. There are those who clearly are living out Christ-centered lives; no matter what the circumstance, they thrive. They have a passion to learn, pray, serve God, and to be a light by mentoring others along the way. They freely share their faith and have a desire to interact with others who are searching for answers about God, life and death.

Mixed among them are Christians, who are nice people, but have little passion for Christ. Their conversations and lives generally do not reflect Christ. Many put in our time by attending church and giving money to worthy organizations, but that is about it. Their desire to learn more about the Christian faith and about God is minimal, and the thought of praying is something they don't do because, frankly, they don't know how! Most of these people are the way they are because they have not been taught how to have a strong faith in Jesus that is life changing. Many of these people long for a more meaningful relationship, but continue the way they are because no one offers them another choice.

Why the difference, and what can we do if we do not want to be passive about our faith? Is there hope for us? Yes, absolutely!

Becoming a Christian who has an authentic and active faith in Jesus does not mean having a strict religious regimen in order to try hard to be like Christ. Being an active Christian is also not a hobby or a once a week event, and it has nothing to do with keeping rules and regulations. It is not about abandoning the intellect and it is anything but signing up for a life of boredom. It is all about God's grace and His gift of the Holy Spirit couple with our desire to get to know God in a real way. When we make that choice to believe in and trust Jesus with our everyday lives then God will be faithful to speak into us through the Holy Spirit, who lives in all those who believe (Ephesians 1:13-14). The eternal Holy Spirit changes us from the inside out as He actively lives in us to guide, teach, convict and even pray for us (Acts 1:8, John 14:16, Romans 8:9). Because God is eternal, His Spirit will never run dry. Within the Spirit, and now within all who believe, is an endless flow of His power, His love and His grace that has prepared us to be a great blessing to others whom we have yet to meet.

Getting to know God is like any other relationship: the more time you spend together the more you learn about Him and the more you will grow to trust and love Him. Spending time with God on a daily basis helps us begin to see how much He is involved in our lives. We will begin to have insight into people and problems that we have not had before. When difficult situations come up, the peace we have knowing God is in us and will walk with us through it all makes things so much easier. When we choose to spend time getting to know Him, He changes the desires of our hearts. He teaches us truth and conforms us, as broken as we are, to become more like Him! It is truly a wonderful thing! All this because it is Jesus' desire that we have life and have it abundantly (John 10:10)!

This much I know about for sure: life does not work without Him. We were created in the image of God to walk with Him, to learn from Him, to be transformed through Him and to be used by Him to bring others into a saving understanding of Jesus Christ. He has given us a new life, His life.

Because we are all created in His image, we were built to communicate with the King of kings. We are created unique and different from all other people ever created. Different looks, temperaments, personalities, and gifts. Sadly, so often within the Christian community, we sometimes not so gently, force people to follow a performance model that does not work for all Christ bearers. Some are shy and not as excitable as others, and that is a good thing because God has other things in mind for these people that do not require high-energy responses. They are Christ followers to the core even though they do not get excited during praise and worship time, do not surround themselves with Christian friends, and would never consider praying out loud in a group setting. So often these people never find their niche because they think that God only uses the more excitable ones. The good news for the quiet or shy believer is that He does not expect you to be anything other than who He has created you to be. God loves authenticity. He is not into performance, but loves for His children to praise and worship Him as directed by the Holy Spirit. All His children matter to Him—and yes, He has created us with purpose to live out Christ in all of life. Who knows, you might be surprised at what He will do!

Although we are very different from one another, if we have believed Jesus to be our Savior, we are His children. For us to live a full life and shine Christ's light, we have to sharpen our communicate skills with God by learning how to listen to His voice and follow Him. We also need to learn how to trust Him in all of life—in the big and little things. God promises that He will finish His work in us!

"And I am sure of this, that he who began a good work in you will bring it to completion at the day of Jesus Christ" (Philippians 1:6).

Spending time with God means learning how to communicate with Him in real everyday conversation. Prayer is talking with God, not in the King James English, but in our own way of speaking. Prayer is about thanking God for who He is, for who we are and for all that He has given us. God wants to know what is on our heart and He wants us to know what is on His. He desires that we understand how much He loves and thinks about us. We are praying to God, not Santa, so our conversation goes way beyond an ask list. Prayer is about getting to know God one on one. Ask God to lead you through your prayer. Come to Him as you are, no matter if you have really messed up. Be honest with God about what your struggles and ask Him to forgive you for whatever He is prompting you to say. He is sympathetic and is so pleased that you have come to Him. If there is something that you want to confess to Him, then do so—and don't forget to thank Him for forgiving and forgetting that sin!

One way to talk to God is to pray through the Scriptures. I love the Psalms and will pick one or part of one and read it back to God, thanking Him and asking Him questions along the way. What is so great about the Holy Spirit is that He is an amazing teacher and will explain things that we don't understand. A study Bible with footnotes about the verses you are reading is an added help for learning more about a passage. I am not talking about reading for hours; do whatever works for you. Some suggestions that you might start with are Psalm 23, 139, 100, 40, 27, 91 or any others. Sometimes I will read a line, other times a verse, and sometimes the whole Psalm. Reading through the New Testament is wonderful. God blesses those who seek Him with wisdom, revelation of the knowledge in Him as we work our way through these books (Ephesians 1:17-20). You won't run out of material to read, I promise. There are some wonderful Scripture based devotional books out there that will help also. No matter how we pray, the more time we spend praying, the more we will desire His will rather than our own. I guess that is because the more time spent with each other, the more we can learn to trust Him! Don't let your time with God become a check on your to do list. Remember, God wants your heart, mind, soul and strength—not a performance!

You do not have to grow in your faith by yourself. Our God is a relational God who desires that we spend time with other Christ followers, learning from one another and encouraging each other in our walks with God. When Christians pray, share, learn, laugh, and work together, we function the way God designed the Church to be. This group can also serve as a support to help those in the group and others, with spiritual, financial and physical needs. Yes, this call to community also includes you who do not like to be in groups. Once you try it, God will bless it, and may even change your mind about meeting with other Christ followers—so watch out!

When we become Christ followers, most of us understand, to some degree, the sacrifice that Christ made for us. He gave up His position in Heaven to become one of us, He knew that He was coming to this earth to die for the sins of the world. The fact that God died for the sins of those He created is close to impossible to fully understand—amazing love.

"Have this mind among yourselves, which is yours in Christ Jesus, who, though he was in the form of God, did not count equality with God a thing to be grasped, but emptied himself, by taking the form of a servant, being born in the likeness of men. And being found in human form, he humbled himself by becoming obedient to the point of death, even death on a cross" (Philippians 2:5-8).

We see Jesus praying in the Garden of Gethsemane in great anguish over what was about to happen. As a suffering servant, Christ could have refused to go to the cross or refused to come under the will of the Father, both of which He chose to do. No human could even begin to know how painful this was for Jesus and His Father. The anguish associated with this act has no words, but Jesus did it anyway because of His love for us.

"And he withdrew from them about a stone's throw, and knelt down and prayed, saying, 'Father, if you are willing, remove this cup from me. Nevertheless, not my will, but yours, be done.' And there appeared to him an angel from heaven, strengthening him. And being in an agony he prayed more earnestly; and his sweat became like great drops of blood falling down to the ground" (Luke 22:41-44).

Jesus was sentenced to death, was willingly taken to be beaten, and willingly whipped beyond recognition.

"And they stripped him and put a scarlet robe on him, and twisting together a crown of thorns, they put it on his head and put a reed in his right hand. And kneeling before him, they mocked him, saying, 'Hail, King of the Jews!' And they spit on him and took the reed and struck him on the head. And when they had mocked him, they stripped him of the robe and put his own clothes on him and led him away to crucify him" (Matthew 27:28-31).

Jesus died on the cross. He fulfilled his promise that he made to Abraham 2,000 years earlier, proving Himself to be faithful to His word. He gave his life to pay the penalty for the sins of the world.

"Surely he has borne our grief and carried our sorrows; yet we esteemed him stricken, smitten by God, and afflicted. But he was pierced for our transgressions; he was crushed for our iniquities; upon him was the chastisement that brought us peace, and with his wounds we are healed" (Isaiah 53:4-5).

None of us can begin to comprehend what Jesus really did for us on the cross that caused such pain, suffering and sacrifice. But this we do understand: the very least we can do in response to the love He demonstrated to us, is to love and follow Him, even sacrificially when asked. It is a privilege to obey Him because it is our way to thank Him and honor Him as our Savior and Lord.

Because of the price that was paid on the cross for our sins, God is extremely serious that we obey Him. Living out our life with God in us must be taken seriously. The word "believe" holds in it our desire to obey. Jesus cannot be Lord if we continue to do our own thing. You cannot have Jesus and not obey; God does not leave that option open.

"The Father loves the Son and has given all things into his hand. Whoever believes in the Son has eternal life; whoever does not obey the Son shall not see life, but the wrath of God remains on him" (John 3:35-36).

God has not called us to keep a list of dos and don'ts, or a list of all the good things we have done. What He wants is for us to worship Him by the way we live. No one has said it is easy. However, the joy that we have in living with Christ goes beyond human expression. Jesus' instructions are short and to the point, and they will not only change us, but our world as well!

"And behold, a lawyer stood up to put him to the test, saying, 'Teacher, what shall I do to inherit eternal life?' He said to him, 'What is written in the Law? How do you read it?' And he answered, 'You shall love the Lord your God with all your heart and with all your soul and with all your strength and with all your mind, and your neighbor as yourself.' And he said to him, 'You have answered correctly; do this, and you will live'" (Luke 10:27-28).

CHAPTER TWENTY-ONE

MOVE AHEAD

Chapter 21: Move Ahead

When I trusted Christ to be my Savior, my life changed dramatically. It was like I could not help myself; I could not wipe that smile off my face. I had found what I had been look-ing for all my life, and the joy it brought me was unbelievable and sometimes uncontrollable. I dove into the Scriptures and into biblical resources that would begin to fill that void of truth in my soul. I had an insatiable hunger for knowing God. It was like I had found a cure for death, which I had, that certainly everyone would love to have. Why wouldn't they? This was not good news; this was great news!

Soon after becoming a Christ follower, I won a golf tour-nament and was expected to give the normal "thank you" speech after receiving the trophy. So, after thanking the com-mittee and fellow competitors, I said something like, "I have got to tell you about someone who has changed my life and can change your life too. It's Jesus! Seriously, He is amazing. If you want to know more about Him, ask me, and we can talk about it during our lunch." What I actually felt like doing was to individually grab them by the shoulders and tell them, "He is alive and He loves you!" but I thought better of it. I was sure that many would want to learn more, why not? To my surprise, that was not the case. There was one, however, a sportscaster from the local TV station who approached me and said that he would like to hear more. The two of us had lunch together and soon after he also placed his trust in Jesus.

Through the years, I have since learned to outwardly con-trol myself, but inwardly, I still want to shout from the hills to any who might listen: "God loves you and has an amazing plan for your life. Believe it because it is true! See for yourselves!" The times we live in are scary and disheartening: Marriages are falling apart, children are struggling as they are constantly being bombarded with conflicting worldviews, the economy is unstable, and the government is in constant turmoil. Depres-sion and suicides are at an all time high. If ever there was a time when people needed Jesus, it is now. Why then, are so many of the people that God has put in our lives deaf to the message of the good news of great joy for all people? Is it because they do not see the love and compassion of Jesus consistently lived out in those who claim to be His children? Has anyone been speaking God's love and forgiveness into them with words and action? Might it be that they have misconceptions about God that keep them from finding truth and they don't know anyone with whom to talk? Perhaps it is because they know they have messed up and are convinced God hates them and wants nothing to do with them.

The real question is: are you content in letting others suffer with unbelief without doing anything to help them? If your answer is "No, I am not content with that", then how can you and I most effectively get the message out to these people? Is there a way? Yes, nothing is impossible with God. Especially when He has called **all** of us to go beyond our own boundaries, our own fears, our own comfort, and our own plans. Christians have been given the charge to be light bearers, ambassadors, and missionaries beginning in their own homes, communities and work places. From a human perspective, it is a daunting task. However, with a willing heart and the Holy Spirit living in us, God will reach those who are broken and lost without hope. It's His job and He loves it!

"And he said to them, 'Go into all the world and proclaim the gospel to the whole creation'" (Mark 16:15).

For most all of us, the idea of going beyond our own church and into our community of friends and co-workers may seem scary and bit foreign. But keeping our faith to ourselves is not what Jesus has designed for us. Nancy Pearcy writes in *Total Truth*, "Our lives are often fractured and fragmented, with our faith firmly locked into the private realm of church and family where it rarely has a chance to inform our life and work in the public realm. The aura of worship dissipates after Sunday and we unconsciously absorb secular attitudes the rest of the week. We inhabit two separate worlds, navigating a sharp divide between our religious life and ordinary life."[1] It is no wonder that this country and our communities have grown cold toward God.

Understanding the foundation of the Christian faith is critical on many counts. If we are students of our faith, we will be effective communicators of what it means to be a Christian and how one can live Christ out in all of life. Knowing what we believe and how we can be sure it is truth is important not just for our own affirmation, but for sharing it with others as well. Having a good grasp of what other religions embrace is hugely important because it enables us to intelligently discuss issues with others of different faiths. Through rational discourse, we can teach and challenge others through friendly discussions and exchanges, without getting defensive and speaking about things we do not know. Admitting we have no clue how to answer some questions is a good thing. It is refreshing to have a discussion with a Christian who admittedly does not have all the answers!

If you are thinking at this point that you believe in Christ as your Savior but are terrified with the thought of actually talking to others about Jesus, you are in good company. The greatest biblical leaders that God handpicked to speak on His behalf felt the same way. Moses was asked by God Himself to go and speak to the Egyptians. *"But Moses said to the Lord, 'Oh, my Lord, I am not eloquent, either in the past or since you have spoken to your servant, but I am slow of speech and of tongue.' Then the Lord said to him, 'Who has made man's mouth? Who makes him mute, or deaf, or seeing, or blind? Is it not I, the Lord? Now therefore go, and I will be with your mouth and teach you what you shall speak.' But he said, 'Oh, my Lord, please send someone else'" (Exodus 4:10-13).* God sent with Moses his brother Aaron, but Moses was the still the one God spoke through.

God had a similar conversation with His prophet Jeremiah. *"Now the word of the Lord came to me, saying, 'Before I formed you in the womb I knew you, and before you were born I consecrated you; I appointed you a prophet to the nations.' Then I said, 'Ah, Lord God! Behold, I do not know how to speak, for I am only a youth.' But the Lord said to me, 'Do not say, 'I am only a youth'; for to all to whom I send you, you shall go, and whatever I command you, you shall speak. Do not be afraid of them, for I am with you to deliver you, declares the Lord.' Then the Lord put out his hand and touched my mouth" (Jeremiah 1:4-9).*

What astounds me is that after the death and resurrection of Christ, God chose to no longer reside in the temple in the Holy of Holies. Ray Vanderlaan tells the story of a Christian Jew who said that when Christ was resurrected, the curtain in the temple that separated man from God ripped from top to bottom. Not only did that mean that people now had direct access to God, but also that God had left the Ark of the Covenant and came into the world. He could have chosen to live anywhere. There are some beautiful churches and cathedrals and vistas throughout the world, but God did not want to live there. Instead He chose to live in those who believe in Him, that is you and me, and through us, the world![2]

"No one after lighting a lamp puts it in a cellar or under a basket, but on a stand, so that those who enter may see the light" (Luke 11:33).

If you have read much of the New Testament, you have read the works of the Apostle Paul. He knew that if God graded on the curve, he would never have been chosen by Him to be His mouthpiece. Paul wrote that he was the worst of sinners but because of God's grace he was deemed by God to be righteous, free from the penalty of sin. Not only did he have a shady past, including killing Christians, he also struggled with his speech. *"And I, when I came to you, brothers, did not come proclaiming to you the testimony of God with lofty speech or wisdom. For I decided to know nothing among you except Jesus Christ and him crucified. And I was with you in weakness and in fear and much trembling, and my speech and my message were not in plausible words of wisdom, but in demonstration of the Spirit and of power, so that your faith might not rest in the wisdom of men but in the power of God"* (1 Corinthians 2:1-5).

"You whom I took from the ends of the earth, and called from its farthest corners, saying to you, 'You are my servant. I have chosen you and not cast you off; fear not, for I am with you; be not dismayed, for I am your God; I will strengthen you, I will help you, I will uphold you with my righteous right hand" (Isaiah 41:9-10).

As you have learned, God trusted a variety of people to write His words into what we now call the Bible. He used people that had a heart for Him and knew His voice as He spoke through the Holy Spirit. God was not concerned about someone's education, social status or if they were prepared for what He was asking them to do. God will wait until we obey Him and then He will equip us. If we are willing to trust Him with our lives and are open to being used by Him to bring others to know Him then He will use us—just as we are!

"But he said to me, 'My grace is sufficient for you, for my power is made perfect in weakness.' Therefore I will boast all the more gladly of my weaknesses, so that the power of Christ may rest upon me. For the sake of Christ, then, I am content with weaknesses, insults, hardships, persecutions, and calamities. For when I am weak, then I am strong" (2 Corinthians 12:9-10).

Many subscribe to the idea that all missionaries go to foreign countries to share the good news. If we are believers in Jesus, we too are missionaries. Our mission field is where we live, work and play. What does a missionary look like? Just like you! A missionary is anyone who is a Christ follower. He, the Holy Spirit, is in us all the time—and He is not leaving! One of my greatest fears was that God was going to send me to Africa as a missionary. After a few years of being a Christian, I told God that even if He were to ask me to go to Africa, I would go. To my relief, He quieted that fear and encouraged me to begin to teach my own children about Jesus in my own home. Now, after preparing me in the small things over the years, I have the opportunity to speak to many different people around the world, even in Africa! Yes, I still get nervous. I try to be well prepared but knowing that God has always and will continue to be faithful to bring to the right words, ideas and thoughts that clearly are not from me, gives me peace in speaking for Him. I will say, beyond the work and sacrifice, there is no greater joy than to have God use me to make a difference in in just one person's life!

I had a student come up to me after class to tell me that she could not stay for the small group discussion because she was sick. I told her that of course that was fine to miss her small group and then asked her why she came to class if she was not feeling well. She said that she was invited by a friend to come to the Anchorsaway class because she did not know

Jesus and had some questions that her friend could not answer. She said that within the first few sessions she had put her trust in Jesus as her personal Savior and had become a Christian. Her life change was so evident to her family that they began to question her about what she was learning. She began to teach her mom and dad along with her aunt and uncle what she had learned at Anchorsaway. So, after each session, she would teach her family what she had learned from that week's class. She said they too had become Christ followers. "That's why I just can't miss a class. It means too much to our family and I want to make sure that I get it right." This girl was 18 years old and had no formal training on how to share her faith. She was not apprehensive about telling her parents what had happened to her nor was she putting on an act because it was real. That is what it means have an authentic faith in Jesus. She was lost, met Jesus through a friend, believed, Jesus changed her life for all to see and then she shared with them on how they too could know and trust Him. It's simple, profoundly simple.

Christ said that we will be known by the fruit of our lives. It may begin with a softening of the heart toward God, a new peace we have within us, or maybe a desire to read the Scriptures and pray. This transformation begins in the heart, not in the performance realm. From the moment we become followers of Christ to the day we die, the Holy Spirit is working in us, filing off the rough edges and preparing us to learn to listen to His voice and respond affirmatively to those things that he is calling us to do.

That is why God designed us in His image so that, through us, people could learn about Jesus just by living and working with us. Hopefully they will see Christ's love, encouragement, hope and integrity in us. Through a friendship with us, they can begin to understand what it means to trust someone who truly cares about them. It will also give them a chance to share from their heart about their life, thoughts and their questions about God. This is what it means to be a light bearer. This is what it means to be an authentic Christian who has a heart that beats for God.

"And Jesus went throughout all the cities and villages, teaching in their synagogues and proclaiming the gospel of the king-

dom and healing every disease and every affliction. When he saw the crowds, he had compassion for them, because they were harassed and helpless, like sheep without a shepherd. Then he said to his disciples, 'The harvest is plentiful, but the laborers are few; therefore pray earnestly to the Lord of the harvest to send out laborers into his harvest'" (Matthew 9:35-38).

In Revelation 21:1-5 Jesus talks about a time in the future where there will be no more sadness, no death, no pain or suffering. It is a time where God will make all things new. Today, we are reminded in the news and through those with whom we interact on a daily basis, that this world needs hope, encouragement, and healing that can only come from Jesus. He begged the question over 2000 years ago and it is still applicable today: Where are the laborers? If you are a child of God, then you are a laborer. Are you willing and are you ready to go? God working in you may require you to write someone a letter of encouragement or perhaps one of asking forgiveness, to engage in a conversation with someone who you know is hurting, to visit someone in the hospital or to really pray for someone when they ask you to pray. Maybe it will be to quietly walk away from those who are gossiping. A simple kind greeting or a pat on the back might make someone's day. Perhaps it will involve you speaking to some guys on an airplane when all you want to do is sleep! Some of your encounters may want to ask you some questions about your faith: How do you know that Christianity is not a hoax? Who is this Jesus to whom you pray? Does it really matter what god you worship? If God is a good God, why did He allow His Son to die? Is the Bible true?

Hopefully, now these questions will not go unanswered! I pray that you will continue to grow in your faith and that your life will reflect the One True God who loves you and has called you to go into your world and let His light shine for all to see. Are you willing?

"And I heard the voice of the Lord saying, 'Whom shall I send, and who will go for us?' Then I said, 'Here I am! Send me.' And he said, 'Go...'" (Isaiah 6:8).

Endnotes

CHAPTER 2: THE SEARCH

1. Barna Group. State of the Church Series. 2011.
2. Ibid.
3. Merriam-Webster's Collegiate Dictionary (10th ed.) (1993). Springfield, MA: Merriam-Webster.
4. Chapell, Bryan. Holiness by Grace. Wheaton: Crossway, 2001.

CHAPTER 3: ALARMING REALITY

1. Barna Group. State of the Church Series. 2011.

CHAPTER 5: FIGHT CLUB

1. Kaufmann, Walter. The Portable Neitzsche, 1954.
2. Carattini, Jill. Ravi Zacharias International Ministries, [Slice 1451] Matters of the Heart, (29 June 2007).

CHAPTER 6: OH MY GOD

1. Lewis, C.S. The Problem of Pain. New York: MacMillan Publishing Co., 1978.
2. Ibid.

CHAPTER 7: I AM

1. Tozer, A. W. The Knowledge of the Holy. San Franciso: Harper Collins, 1961.
2. White, James. A Brief Description of the Trinity. Alpha and Omega Ministries. 4 April 2005.
3. Grudem, Wayne. Systematic Theology. Zondervan, 1995.

CHAPTER 8: I DOUBT IT

1. The Wycliffe Bible Commentary, Electronic Database. Copyright 1962 by Moody Press.
2. Brussell, Eugene E. Websters New World Dictionary of Quotable Definitions. Prentice Hall Trade, 1988.

3. Chesterton, G.K. What's Wrong with the World. Dover Publications, 2012.

4. Kennedy, James. Why I Believe. Thomas Nelson, 1999.

5. Zacharias, Ravi. Cries of the Heart. Thomas Nelson, 1998.

CHAPTER 9: THE I OF THE STORM

1. Sagan, Carl. Cosmos. New York: Ballantine Books, 1985.

2. Dawkins, Richard. The New Humanist, from the Journalist Press Association, v107, no. 2.

3. Russell, Bertrand. Why I Am Not a Christian and Other Essays on Religion and Related Subjects. Barlow Press, 2008.

4. Voltaire, Francois. Dictionnaire Philosophique, 1964.

CHAPTER 10: LOVE LETTER

1. McDowell, Josh. Evidence that Demands a Verdict, vol. 1. Nashville: Thomas Nelson Publishers, 1999.

2. The information in this section was adapted from page 14 of "Discovering the Bible: What it is, how we got it, and how to use it", the publication accompanying the video series, Discovering the Bible. Produced by Gateway Films, Worchester, PA. Christian History Institute, 1996.

3. Greenlee, J. Harold. Introduction to New Textual Criticism. Grand Rapids: Wm. B. Eerdman's Publishing Co., 1964.

CHAPTER 11: SCIENCE AND NUMBERS

1. A few religious books contain a handful of vague or silly "prophecies". For example, Buddhist scripture contains the following, "At that time happiness, like beholding the sun, in this Tibet will occur, I think" – Prophecy of the Fifth Karmapa, Deshin Shekpa. The Koran contains a prophecy that Mohammed will return to Mecca, which of course is self-fulfilling! The Mormon "Doctrine and Covenants" scripture contains some prophecies that utterly failed (see "One Nation Under Gods", Richard Abanes, 2002, p. 461-467 for a long list of failed prophecies by Joseph Smith).

2. Stoner, Peter. Science Speaks. Chicago: Moody Press, 1958.

3. Missler, Chuck. "Footprints of the Messiah". Audiocassette. Koinonia House.

4. Nelson, Glueck. Rivers in the Desert, 1960.

5. Jones, Scott. The Veracity of the Old Testament: A Scientific Validation, 1997.

6. Eusebius. Ecclesiastical History III.39, found in McDowell's, Evidence that Demands a Verdict.

7. Flavius Josephus. The Works of Josephus, translated by William Whiston. Peabody, MA: Hendrickson Publishers, Inc.

CHAPTER 12: NOT WHAT I EXPECTED

1. Lewis, C.S. Mere Christianity. San Francisco: Harper Collins, 1952.

2. Vine, W.E. An Expository Dictionary. Thomas Nelson, 1996.

3. Hale, Thomas. The Applied New Testament Commentary. Colorado Springs: Victory Books, 1996.

4. McDowell, Josh. Evidence That Demands a Verdict vol.1. Nashville: Thomas Nelson Publishers, 1979.

5. Kennedy, D. James. Why I Believe. Thomas Nelson [Revised Edition], 1999.

CHAPTER 13: NO FREE LUNCH

1. Vander Laan, Ray. Abram's Animal Ceremony in Genesis 15: An Exegesis of Genesis 15:7-21. (Resource is available under "Going Deeper" Chapter 13: No Free Lunch)

CHAPTER 14: FORWARDING ADDRESS

1. Derek R. Moore, "Galatians 4:1-9: The Use and Abuse of Parallels", The Evangelical Quarterly, vol. LXI/No. 3 (1989), p. 216.

CHAPTER 15: A BEAUTIFUL LIE

1. Thanks to Andrew Heister, Jeff Myers, and Mark Cahill for the four deadly questions which have been used for many years in the teaching at Summit Ministries (Colorado Springs, CO). As a frequent educator at Summit, Mark Cahill effectively explains these penetrating questions in this book – Mark Cahill, One Thing You Can't Do in Heaven (Bartlesville, OK: Genesis Publishing Group, 2004).

2. Lewis, C.S. Mere Christianity. San Francisco: Harper Collins, 1952.

Nancy Fitzgerald

CHAPTER 16: CHARADES

1. Barna Group. Teenager Series. 15 April 2005.

2. Grudem, Wayne. Systematic Theology: An Introduction to Biblical Doctrine. Grand Rapids: Zondervan, 1994. See also Merrill F. Unger, and William White, Jr., Nelsons Expository Dictionary of the Old Testament, W.E. Vine, Merrill F. Unger, and William While, Jr., Vine's Complete Expository Dictionary of Old and new Testament Words (Nashville, TN: Thomas Nelson Publishers, 1996).

CHAPTER 18: IDENTITY THEFT

1. McDowell, Josh and Steward, Don. Understanding the Cults. San Bernardino: Here's Life Publishers, Inc, 1982.

2. Tanner, Jerald and Sandra. 3,913 Changes in the Book of Mormon. Salt Lake City: Utah Lighthouse Ministry, 1996.

3. Tanner, Jerald and Sandra. Mormonism – Shadow or Reality? Salt Lake City: Utah Lighthouse Ministry, Fifth Edition, 1987.

4. Joseph Smith, Journal of Discourses, Volume 6, (1844) 3-5. Also see: Bob Witte, Where Does It Say That? (Grand Rapids: Gospel Truths)

5. Joseph Smith, Journal of Discourses, Volume 6, (1844) 8. Also see: Brigham Young, Journal of Discourses, Volume 8 (1860) 268.

6. Joseph Fielding Smith, Doctrines of Salvation, Volume 1, 39. Also see: Jerald and Sandra Tanner, Mormonism – Shadow or Reality? (Salt Lake City: Utah Lighthouse Ministry, Fifth Edition, 1987.

7. Grudem, Wayne. Systematic Theology: And Introduction to Biblical Doctrine. Grand Rapids: Zondervan, 1994.

8. Orson Pratt, The Seer (1853) 172.

9. Bruce McConkie, The Mortal Messiah, Volume 4, 434.

10. Orson Pratt, The Seer (1853) 158. Also see: Bob Witte, Where Does It Say That? (Grand Rapids, Gospel Truths) 4-7.

11. Bruce McConkie, speech given at BYU devotional (2 March 1982.

12. Book of Mormon, II Nephi 25:23.

13. Joseph Smith, Journal of Discourses, Volume 6, (1844) 3-4. Also see: Bob Witte, Where Does It Say That? (Grand Rapids: Gospel Truths).

14. Joseph Smith, History of the Church, Volume 1, 283.

15. Joseph Fielding Smith, Doctrines of Salvation, Volume 2, 133.

16. Joseph Fielding Smith, Doctrines of Salvation, Volume 2, 183. Also see: Jerald and Sandra Tanner, Mormonism – Shadow or Reality? (Salt Lake City: Utah Lighthouse Ministry, Fifth Edition, 1987) 198-199.

17. Ibid., 93.

18. The Mormon meanings associated with the previous ten different doctrinal expressions come from Agusta Harting, Families Against Cults of Indiana, 26 April 2005 (see familiesagainstcults.org)

CHAPTER 19: THE GAMBLE

1. Barna Group. State of the Church Series. 2011.

2. Vine's Expository Dictionary of New Testament Words.

CHAPTER 21: MOVE AHEAD

1. Pearcey, Nancy. Total Truth. Crossway, 2008.

2. "That the World May Know", Focus on the Family Films. Colorado Springs, 1997.

Appendix

Your Turn

Thank you for traveling on this journey with us. Our deepest desire is that you will start or continue living a culture changing life with a Christian worldview as your compass. Our hope is that your life will reflect what Christ has done, and is doing in you each and every day. We challenge you to always be ready to share the truth of Christ and the life that He offers, to anyone who asks.

Now that you have gone through the *Unanswered: Smoke, Mirrors, and God* study, you are in a great position to take what you have learned and teach juniors and seniors in high school with the Anchorsaway Christian worldview curriculum. This curriculum is designed to be taught by adults as a community study in a home setting. It is for anyone who is either questioning their faith or wants to deepen their faith with solid answers from history, science, the Bible and scholars who are experts in their respective fields. Not only will Anchorsaway students learn with clarity about the hope they have, but they will also be armed to answer questions about their faith with confidence in an unbelieving world!

The curriculum covers 21 major questions that are listed below. It can be taught by a trained teacher or through videos. If you are interested, please go to our website for more information. On our site, you can learn more about who we are and even sign up for an online teacher training class. Our website is anchorsaway.org.

Chapters offered in the Anchorsaway Curriculum:

1. What is the Christian Worldview?
2. What are the Five Major Worldviews?
3. Who is God?
4. Is the Bible Reliable?
5. Was Jesus Christ Resurrected? Why Does it Matter?
6. Is Jesus Christ God? What is the Trinity?
7. What is a Christian? Am I One?
8. Did Life Just Happen or Were We Created?
9. Who is the god of Islam?
10. What is the Big Picture of God's Redemption of Man?
11. Who is Satan and How Does He Work?
12. What is a Cult?
13. Why Don't the Jews Believe in Jesus?
14. How Does God View the Homosexual?
15. What are the Moral Implications of Bioethics?
16. What is the Christian Role in Cultural Reconciliation?
17. What are the Biblical Principles to Wise Financial Planning?
18. How can I become a Leader Who Influences Culture for Christ?
19. Why Does God allow Suffering?
20. How Do I Make Good Life choices?
21. What are the Keys to Building Healthy Relationships?

Notes

Unanswered

Notes

Notes

Notes